THE TAO
OF
THOMAS AQUINAS

THE TAO
OF
THOMAS AQUINAS

FIERCE WISDOM FOR HARD TIMES

MATTHEW FOX

THE TAO OF THOMAS AQUINAS
FIERCE WISDOM FOR HARD TIMES

iUniverse books may be ordered through booksellers or by contacting:

iUniverse
1663 Liberty Drive
Bloomington, IN 47403
www.iuniverse.com
1-800-Authors (1-800-288-4677)

Scriptural translations are my own (ably assisted by Fr. Bede Griffiths) directly from Aquinas's translations of the Bible.

This book is available in e-book form in February, 2020. And in audio format in March.

ISBN: 978-1-5320-9341-8 (sc)
ISBN: 978-1-5320-9342-5 (e)

Library of Congress Control Number: 2020901736

Print information available on the last page.

iUniverse rev. date: 01/30/2020

Praise for The Tao of Thomas Aquinas

What a wonderful book! Only Matt Fox could bring to life the wisdom and brilliance of Aquinas with so much creativity. *Tao of Thomas Aquinas* is a masterpiece.

--Caroline Myss, author of *Anatomy of the Spirit*

Matthew Fox's exciting book on Thomas Aquinas breaks new ground in appreciating the great saint's spiritual depths and practical wisdom. As Fox indicates, citing a great historian with whom he studied, Aquinas's spirituality is "everywhere" in his work because he is so attuned to the sacredness of life itself and of nature in all its diverse and wonderful beauty--including human nature and its creativity. Aquinas comes through as a real brother to Francis of Assisi and a real champion for our times as humanity faces eco destruction and massive extinctions. This handbook offers a guide for all who want to stand up, be counted and make a difference.

--Richard Rohr, OFM, Living School for Center of Action and Contemplation, author, *Divine Dance*

In the future, when we look back at the individuals who had the greatest impact on Christian thinking in the early 21st century, I believe that Matthew Fox will be among those at the top of the list. He has not only gone far in rattling conservative dogma, but he has done it from a place deeply rooted in scripture and tradition. His vision of a more contemplative, compassionate, and social-justice-oriented Christianity is exactly what is needed for our faith to survive and grow--at once nourishing the world and being in dialogue with other spiritual traditions.

Fox has a special ability to recontextualize the deep mystical wisdom of the spiritual masters of the church in a way that makes them urgently relevant for our times. This is exactly what he has done with Thomas Aquinas in his new book--showing us how this medieval, Dominican scholar has much to teach us about mysticism, modern psychology, the environmental movement, science, and social justice. Fox has once again taken some of the gems of the Christian tradition and made them sparkle anew.

> --Paul Engler, founding director of Center for the Working Poor and co-author, *This Is An Uprising*

This thrilling, exalted, fierce, sublime book by our greatest and wisest living Christian prophet reveals Thomas Aquinas not only as the Bach of Christian mystics, boundlessly and groundedly creative, majestic and pragmatic—but also as the most inspired and vibrant possible companion for all sacred activists now struggling to birth a new world. No one but Matthew Fox could have pulled off so magical and necessary a resurrection. Whatever path you are on, read this book and be renewed by its illumined passion for the titanic work ahead.

> —Andrew Harvey, author of *The Hope* and *Turn Me to Gold: 108 Translations of Kabir.*

In my 20s I encountered Thomas Aquinas while studying the creation spirituality of Matthew Fox. This turned out to be an event that changed my life forever. It felt like I had discovered a secret energy source, like I was this lonely geologist who had stumbled upon an untapped oil field as vast as Saudi Arabia, but one filled with a psychic form of energy a thousand times more potent than oil or gas. Thomas Aquinas's wisdom supercharged my life and my creativity for decades. You have in your hands the magical switch to the spiritual energy you need to accomplish the great work for which you were created. Nothing can stop you now.

—Brian Thomas Swimme, California Institute of Integral Studies, cosmologist and author of *The Universe Story* (with Thomas Berry) and *Journey of the Universe*

With his characteristic vigor, wit, and startling insight, Matthew Fox reclaims living wisdom from the murky recesses of theology. Who knew that Thomas Aquinas was so extravagantly brimming with a vital blend of earthy reverence and contemplative quietude, blessing the holiness of all that is incarnational while exalting the One that transcends all distinction? May these distilled teachings contribute to mending the torn web of the world.

—Mirabai Starr, author of *God of Love: A Guide to the Heart of Judaism, Christianity and Islam* and *Wild Mercy: Living the Fierce and Tender Wisdom of the Women Mystics*

Matthew Fox's *The Tao of Thomas Aquinas: Fierce Wisdom for Hard Times* is a little book that asks big questions. It brings the work of Aquinas to the fundamental challenges and questions of our time: How can we rediscover our place in the cosmos? How can we be joyful in difficult times? How can our spiritual lives serve to bring forth a more just and sustainable culture for all rather than salvation for a few? This book points out that we need the energy of today's youth, but we also need the cosmic mysticism of Aquinas—and Matthew Fox.

> —Theodore Richards, author of *Creatively Maladjusted* and *The Great Re-Imagining: Spirituality in an Age of Apocalypse*

This is a beautiful and important book. Once again, Matthew Fox manages to bring Thomas Aquinas into the 21st century and invites us all to the conversation. At a time when our very future is threatened by greed, despair, and the threat of extinction, Aquinas's timeless wisdom, so brilliantly illuminated by Fox, offers a roadmap for spirituality and action—and these teachings are more relevant and needed now than ever before.

> —Adam Bucko, co-author of *Occupy Spirituality* and *The New Monasticism*

In this delightful book, Matthew Fox expresses the radical vision and rapturous heart of the historically misunderstood Thomas Aquinas who speaks often a child-like, brilliant and clear metaphysic of cosmic love. This is a timely book for both the old and the young alike in our culture of suspicion and cynicism. In our age of weaponized words and rapid climate change, young people everywhere are invited to drink from a common stream of wisdom, a Tao, both cool and clear. The sheer wonder of the scientist and the awe of the mystic may meet in the middle of this great bridge of revelation. For the heartbeat of the universe is the heartbeat of God--an exuberant celebration of joy, an ecstatic, drunken dance of love.

> --Matthew Syrdal, author, speaker and Co-founder of Seminary of the Wild

I am awake after reading this remarkable book, and I believe readers who take time to peruse it carefully will awaken to the grandeur of the universe, a cosmos that, according to Aquinas, is the most excellent thing that exists. As readers awaken to the banquet of Fox's newest book (certainly one of his best) a new creation emerges through a "second resurrection" of companioning souls, each in a new creation of "superbeauty," a "fourfold beauty" that aims at personal and global healing.

The Tao of Thomas Aquinas is a gift of supreme thankfulness and praise from the pen of a true Doctor of the Church whose spiritual calling is to *heal us*, with playfulness and celebration, from the stiff teachings and anthropomorphism that historically made Catholic theology sick.

This book is a work of restoration and repairing. It is a work of remarkable revelation and compassion—a redemption of Aquinas from the rational prison he was caged in for 800 years! Fox has freed Aquinas from bondage, liberated his true voice, and given us his grapes of spiritual glory to return us each to our true humanity, before it is too late.

—Steven B. Herrmann, PhD, Jungian analyst and author of *Spiritual Democracy*

Matthew Fox brings Thomas Aquinas to life in a way that transcends intellectual arguments. There is a deep love for Aquinas here, a profound appreciation for the way Thomas delighted in divine freedom and goodness spilling over into creation, instilling an exuberance within creation that awakens within us a desire for beauty, wholeness, and the deepening of love: a creation drunk with beauty and wisdom. . . . Thomas's God soars like the wind beneath our feet, propelling us on to more beauty and truth—a God who is a *living* God, active and alive in our midst, in our cells and bodies, a God breathing new life into everything that exists. What else could religion be but one long continuous act of gratitude. . .?

This is a beautiful book, a book written by one who fell in love with Thomas Aquinas as a young scholar and whose love has never ceased. As a result, the author brings this great medieval theologian's mystical vision into a living reality.

> —from the foreword by Ilia Delio, OFM, author of *The Unbearable Wholeness of Being* and *The Emergent Christ*

Matthew Fox has condensed the deep and complex theology of Thomas Aquinas into delicious bites of wisdom, riffing on key quotations from this medieval churchman who dared to introduce Aristotle's pagan science to Christian Europe, and serving up the choicest morsels with their relevance to twenty-first-century life.

> —Nancy Abrams, author of *View from the Center of the Universe* and *A God That Could Be Real: Spirituality, Science, and the Future of Our Planet*

Matt Fox rescues Aquinas from academia by gleaning wisdom, poetry, and beauty from writings often overlooked. The book presents in easy-to-understand, brief chapters with titles using Aquinas's own words that entice a waking up to investigation, reflection, and conversation. He places Aquinas among a lineage of giants who have something to say to a world in need of a courageous and prophetic boldness. This book can be considered an introduction to the deep questioning and seeking of truth that one finds everywhere in Aquinas.

The use of the word *Tao* references an East/West convergence so needed today in our efforts to bring together action and contemplation, the mystical and the prophetic. Often letting Aquinas speak for himself, the author brings both respect for Aquinas and his lineage and Matt's own scholarship from his years as my Dominican brother. Threats to the earth as we know it and other consequential matters require the efforts of all who seek a spirituality deep and engaging that leads to compassionate action.

Fox refers to this, his latest book, as his "short Aquinas book." It will surely become a straightforward and useful reference for young activists and their mentors whom Matt has in mind. It is easy to imagine it carried in backpacks to wherever its wisdom is needed.

—Br. Joseph Kilikevice, OP, Shem Center for Interfaith Spirituality, Oak Park, Illinois

Thomas Aquinas, like many sages and prophets, has often had his message watered down to the point that the potency of his words is drowned out of existence. However, in this timely work, Matthew Fox has revived Aquinas for our time and given him a framework that allows all of us to recognize that this message is the instrument that will give our weary world a new song of liberation.

While reading through this work, I felt that a great saint (whose work I have enjoyed reading in the past) was speaking directly to me in my current context — a reality that proves Aquinas is speaking wisdom for our times.

I experienced a deep sense of being affirmed while reading through this book. I realized that through the words of Aquinas, my generation *(millennials)* was being granted permission (by a saint!) not only to claim our rightful place as prophets but also to wholeheartedly embrace our identities as the beloved of God.

Aquinas—whether he knew it or not—testifies to the life expressions of many young adults all over this world who have been acting upon the inner tug of Spirit to move forward in daring to build a radically different world where justice is the foundation, elitism is no more, and tenderness is our culture.

Who knew Thomas Aquinas, a medieval theologian and philosopher, was such a revolutionary?! Can we also dare to dwell in our innate goodness and demand that we be treated as the beloved children of God?

Our marching orders are clear, and the path has been set for us. We do not have the luxury of time to allow external forces to keep us from giving birth to new realities of global justice and cosmic oneness. We must embrace the beautiful wisdom in this book and get to work!

> —from the afterword by Rev. Jerry Maynard, twenty-six-year-old activist

I happily dedicate this book to sacred activists everywhere—and especially the young, who face such a challenging future and deserve deep wisdom from the past (and present) to succeed. May you drink deeply from the wisdom of Thomas Aquinas and, like him, be bold, courageous and creative in thought, spirit, and action.

And to my mentor and brother, Père Marie-Dominique Chenu, OP, student and scholar of Thomas Aquinas, who named the tradition of "creation spirituality" that opened doors for so many, and who frequently wrote me signing off with the message "we are brothers in communion of thought."

"Wisdom is able to direct us not only in contemplation but also in action."

—Thomas Aquinas

Contents

Foreword

I was brought up in the rich environment of the Franciscan tradition, with its roots in Francis of Assisi and its deep relational theology developed by Bonaventure and Scotus among others. I learned to navigate the writings of Francis, Bonaventure, and Scotus, and I was trained early on to appreciate that Franciscan theology is primarily affective, a movement of the heart, whereas Thomistic theology is primarily intellectual, a movement of the mind. Bonaventure emphasized the will of God, while Thomas emphasized divine freedom. Bonaventure emphasized love as the nature of God, while Thomas emphasized God as Being—as if being and goodness might be separate and distinct aspects of the divine. Bonaventure devoted thirty-six pages of his first commentary on the *Sentences* to the Trinity, while Thomas only devoted one. Bonaventure was known as a Trinitarian, while Thomas was focused on divine unity. Even their Christologies differed. Bonaventure said that the incarnation took place because of the excess love and mercy of God, an insight developed by Duns Scotus in his doctrine of the primacy of Christ, while Thomas supported Anselm's position—namely, that the reason for the incarnation is the sin of Adam summed up in the Easter Exsultet, "O *felix culpa*! For if Adam had not sinned Christ would not have come."

I developed an image of Thomas Aquinas as an introvert, a thinker more prone to philosophical arguments and intellectual speculation than a one who took seriously the incarnation as the starting point for understanding the God-world relationship. Thomas's God seemed like a Christian version of Auguste Rodin's statue *The Thinker*, present but remote, relational but self-contained, involved but not dependent, interested but only at a distance; a God more transcendent than immanent. I felt sorry for Dominicans, as if they hung their habits on the gates of heaven and committed their lives to a distant God. Franciscans rejoiced in wearing brown habits that would not show the mud and dirt; the Dominican white habit seemed incapable of getting too involved in the cracks of the world where the pus of lepers and bloody tears of beggars filled the crevices.

You can imagine my surprise when Matthew Fox invited me to write a foreword to his new book, *The Tao of Thomas Aquinas.* I did not have the heart to tell him of my biases developed over the years towards the theology of Thomas Aquinas and my absolute commitment to the Franciscan intellectual tradition— not to mention my dismissal of Thomas as a source of stale, static theology. And then I read *The Tao of Thomas*

Aquinas and realized that we can only transcend our biases and judgments by entering the very worlds we reject. I am indebted to Matt for the invitation to write this foreword, for in this rich gemof a book I have found deep resonances with the thought of Bonaventure. Even more, I have discovered a Christian thinker steeped in a dynamic, relational God of overflowing goodness.

Matthew Fox brings Thomas Aquinas to life in a way that transcends intellectual arguments. There is a deep love for Aquinas here, a profound appreciation for the way Thomas delighted in divine freedom and goodness spilling over into creation, instilling an exuberance within creation that awakens within us a desire for beauty, wholeness, and the deepening of love: a creation drunk with beauty and wisdom. God is the fountain and fullness of beauty, diffusing throughout the universe and radiating goodness in a way that escapes the narrowness of human power and control. Thomas's God soars like the wind beneath our feet, propelling us on to more beauty and truth—a God who is a *living* God, active and alive in our midst, in our cells and bodies, a God breathing new life into everything that exists. What else could religion be but one long continuous act of gratitude? Gratitude for the gift of being itself, for the gift of light, stars, galaxies, planets, dirt, amoebas, earthworms, plants, trees, cats, horses, children, and all sorts of human persons. Awakening to the infinite gifts that come from the divine source of exuberant goodness can lead to no other than astonishment and sheer joy of being alive in this moment, as a pure gift of divine love.

Thomas's God is a God of wisdom who delights in play, fun, levity of heart, laughter, the lightness of the Spirit drawing us to imagine, create and invent new ways for wisdom to take hold of us and liberate us from our selfish selves, turning our hearts and minds toward our godly selves, realizing that what we hope for already lies within us. Blessed are those who undergo the first resurrection to new life, for the second resurrection will be an abundance of life beyond our wildest imaginings.

This is a beautiful book, a book written by one who fell in love with Thomas Aquinas as a young scholar and whose love has never ceased. As a result, the author brings this great medieval theologian's mystical vision into a living reality.

Marie-Dominique Chenu, OP, the great Dominican theologian and mentor of Matthew Fox, once described the relationship between the macrocosm (the universe) and the microcosm (the human person) as an "immense zither," an instrumental music of stunning beauty, a harmony created by various strings plucked by the entangled Spirit of God. This is what *The Tao of Thomas Aquinas* gives us: not only the dance of energies that create a vital wholeness but more so a symphony of the strings of love brought to consciousness in the human person who is, in a sense, the conductor of the whole.

I am deeply grateful for the opportunity to read this rich treasure of Thomas's insights and wisdom. And I ask pardon of all Dominicans that I might have offended in the past due to my narrow theological biases. From now on, I shall strive to see the world through the eyes of Thomas—although not to the exclusion of Bonaventure, for I believe these two great lights of the thirteenth century created a stained glass window that allow the sun to radiate in a rich variety of colors and forms. For they both knew that God can be no other than the brilliance of life itself, overflowing, ever-flowing, and forever drawing us into an incomprehensible future fullness of sheer joy.

Ilia Delio
December 8, 2019

Feast of the Immaculate Conception
Villanova University

Preface

While I was writing this book, I became excited about it and described it to others as "a short book on Thomas Aquinas." As I shared draft copies with respected colleagues, many of whose words appear on the "Praise for Tao of Thomas Aquinas" pages, something deeper emerged for me.

Something seemed to speak to me and say: "Aquinas is talking here—one of the greatest geniuses in Western history—he is speaking through you to a new generation, a generation facing profound challenges such as climate change (and climate change denial), spasms of extinction on a scale not seen since the dinosaurs, and the collapse of the modern world amid loss, shadow, and grief. Aquinas wants to speak to this generation out of his depth and wisdom—and you are his mouthpiece, his translator. Give him a microphone, and let him talk about what matters." (Aquinas says "a little knowledge about important things is far more valuable than a lot of knowledge about unimportant things.")

In these pages I have attempted to offer an accessible and succinct platform to hear the heart and mind of this giant thinker, philosopher, scientist, theologian, mystic, and prophet. And to make his wisdom available to many—especially the young.

Thus this handbook of spirituality straight from the mind and heart of my brother Thomas, called "Thomas the Creator" by G. K. Chesterton ninety-seven years ago.

Activists need and deserve a worldview, a cosmology, by which to act, in which to dwell, and to which to return for nourishment when waging battles for a sustainable future. If "ecology is functional cosmology," as Thomas Berry teaches, then we need cosmology in this postmodern time. We need wisdom and not just more knowledge and information. Facts are important, but they do not save us. Wisdom does.

In many ways Aquinas is a central hub in a wheel of philosophical and religious wisdom—he gathers wisdom from philosophers and from the Bible, from theologians and from scientists, from artists and activists. He has been described as having "led a revolution in Christian thought." His thinking offers us all—believers and nonbelievers—a badly needed revolution in consciousness today, one grounded in the sacredness of creation. In this short handbook are insights useful for generations to come.

May Thomas encourage all spiritual warriors and activists from his heart and mind shared in this handbook. Let it grow your vision and your courage.

Take it to prison with you or to school or to church so your love flows, and nondualism and nonviolence blossom into the justice and compassion, the action and the contemplation, for which the human heart longs so deeply.

Matthew Fox
January 15, 2020
Feast of Martin Luther King Jr
Vallejo, California

Introduction
The Boldness of the Man is Amazing

Alice Walker tells us that "hard times require furious dancing." I couldn't agree more. *Hard times also require furious and fierce wisdom, and this is why the courage and truth-seeking of the real Thomas Aquinas deserve an audience today.* Bold ancestor that he is, we must grasp the deep message he offers to bolster our spirits, sharpen our minds, and expand our hearts for compassionate action.

Recently I was invited to speak at a gathering sponsored by the Sierra Club in the Bay Area along with two scientists about the challenges spiritual, scientific, and technological that climate change and species extinction are posing to us all. It was, as one would expect, quite a sobering occasion. After the three of us had spoken, in strode Joanna Macy, who had just celebrated her ninetieth birthday. As she was handed the microphone, she exclaimed: "Isn't it a marvelous time to be alive? What a tremendous gift it is to be invited today to address this crisis from the depths of our humanity and our spiritual lineages?" Her words electrified the audience. Instead of wallowing in despair or sinking into denial or running from our responsibilities, she was inviting us to seize the occasion that history has laid upon us.

I could not agree more. We must call forth the best of our lineages and bring them all to the table, along with scientists and inventors and moral imagination at its fullest. Wendell Berry—farmer, poet, essayist, and prophet of my generation—says that we must "fight the worst with the best."

Clearly what we are facing today is "the worst." The climate emergency that is calling us to change our ways, as well as the freefall of democracy that we see happening all around us, is as bad as it gets. Years ago, Carl Jung predicted that in the Age of Aquarius (in which we are now) evil will no longer be under the table but on top. And he posed the question: Will we have the will to deal with it?

Our times call for boldness. They call for the young to arise to the great task of saving the earth as we know it from collapse—and for the elders to share the stories of wisdom that we carry from our traditions or lineages. Of course, we look many places for the bold wisdom necessary to render us wise and successful. One place to look for wisdom is our ancestors. And Thomas Aquinas (1225–74) is certainly one of those. In response to Wendell Berry's call to "fight the worst with the best," young and future generations deserve to hear the depth and wisdom of Aquinas who brings the "best" into the battle.

Thomas Aquinas, saint and doctor of the church, is one of the greatest geniuses and talented minds to whom the West has ever given birth. Yet, sad to tell, he is not always understood for the bold thinker (and ecumenical champion and creation-centered mystic and lover of creation and justice-oriented prophet) that he was.

Sad to say, movements like "Thomism" have often attracted people who possess far smaller souls than Aquinas, with the result that instead of honoring his breadth and courage and depth of truth-seeking, they often make him over into their pusillanimous image that distort his memory and his sense of intellectual adventure. In the process they have essentially forgotten his amazing contributions to our lives and view of the world, contributions that could help build our strength today as we face unparallel threats to the survival of the earth as we know it and, indeed, to all our relationships.

It is time to rescue Aquinas from Thomism—just as it is time to rescue Jesus from Christianity, Jung from Jungism, and Saint Francis from the birdbath. We humans—and the earth we inhabit—require all the help we can muster, and the brilliant and magnanimous mind and heart of Thomas Aquinas, the wisdom he shares, fill a deep need of our species.

Postmodern times require premodern wisdom. Just as we can benefit profoundly from the wisdom of indigenous peoples today—a wisdom that was trampled on by modern adventurers and philosophers and theologians alike who espoused a philosophy of empire and human narcissism and preoccupation with anthropocentric fears of hell, damnation, and original sin—so, too, can we benefit from the premodern wisdom of Thomas Aquinas. This wisdom begins, as indigenous people do, with a consciousness of the whole—that is, with cosmology. This is how postmodern thinking also begins, as physicist David Bohm confessed: "I am proposing a post-modern physics which begins with the whole." Premodern thinker Aquinas agrees when he reminds us that "The most excellent thing in the universe is not the human; it is the universe itself."

It is rare to encounter a human being of the depth and breadth, love and passion, curiosity and intellectual vigor that Aquinas shared. I recall that when I was writing my major tome on Aquinas, *Sheer Joy: Conversations with Thomas Aquinas on Creation Spirituality*, several years ago I gave a talk at Adrian College in Michigan, a college run by Adrian Dominican sisters. Aquinas had been a Dominican, and I was still one at the time. (Indeed, I realized just this year that I was a Dominican for longer than Aquinas himself—having died young, he was a Dominican for thirty years, whereas I was a Dominican in good standing for thirty-four.)

I shared with the audience some of my findings in researching my new book, which was a first of its kind since I translated many of his works that had never been translated before whether in English, German, Italian, or French. Among these valuable gifts from Aquinas were his first and most mystical book, a commentary on Denys the Areopagite that he wrote at twenty-eight years of age, and his commentaries on the Psalms, Jeremiah, Isaiah, Lamentations, and the Gospels of Matthew and John. It is especially in his biblical commentaries that he reveals his most poetic, mystical, and free-ranging imagination, and it is there that he softens the scholastic framework that formats many of his other works but renders him difficult to grasp by postmodern minds.

After my presentation at Adrian College, an old Dominican sister came up to me with tears running down her cheeks, and she said: "I was instructed in Aquinas and Thomism beginning over fifty years ago. I am so angry—and so sad—that I had to wait over fifty years to hear ideas from Thomas Aquinas that truly move me and inform me for the first time of what made him so great a saint. Why did I have to wait my whole life long to hear these things?"

Why indeed. Because rather than be listened to and

studied for the entirety of his life's work, petty minds landed on a few old philosophical debates or just a few of his writings (always the *Summa Theologiae*) to carry on their diatribes against the modern world in the guise of a rigid orthodox blanket called "Thomism." Père M.-D. Chenu, a great historian and scholar of Aquinas with whom it was my privilege to study during his last year of teaching (spring of 1968 in Paris), said that sixteenth-century Thomists "lost the eminent spiritual equilibrium of their master which would have enabled them to understand, assess and assimilate the rational values of this second Renaissance" (meaning the sixteenth-century reformations). Chenu loved to expound on the "first renaissance" in Europe, the twelfth-century renaissance, which birthed the university, the Gothic revolution in architecture, and Aquinas himself. Chenu continues: "their theology had lost the spirit of daring as well as its original freshness and had forgotten the need of continual rediscovery."[1]

This spirit of "daring and freshness and need for continual rediscovery" are alive and well in the real Thomas Aquinas. Consider the thirty-one chapter titles of this book: Each one is a sentence from Thomas Aquinas. And each one can wake people up. Each title is a meditation in itself, and indeed that is my intention in this book: to let Aquinas speak to us today, especially to the young who are growing up in a postmodern (and not modern) world and who, therefore, whether they know it or not, are hungry for premodern wisdom. Aquinas is a champion, along with indigenous traditions everywhere, of this premodern wisdom. His wisdom is bold and daring.

I have taken a citation from his commentary on John's gospel about Mary Magdalene as the title for this introduction both because Mary Magdalene represents the Divine Feminine, but also because Aquinas praises her boldness and her role as prophet. "The boldness of the woman was amazing."[2] Aquinas, mystic that he was, was also a bold prophet like Mary Magdalene. But something similar could be said of Thomas Aquinas: "the boldness of the man is amazing." He invites us to follow.

Just as Aquinas praises Mary Magdalene for her courage, so I do the same for Aquinas. He was bold; he was daring. He was willing to break radically with the past and to adopt a radical pedagogy—scholasticism—that derived from Islam. In preferring Aristotle to Plato he was turning his back on much of the entire patristic period of theology because so many of the "Fathers of the Church" from the fourth and fifth centuries were Platonists or Neo-Platonists. In many respects, he stood alone against a dualistic establishment centuries in the making. In his non-dualism he was a proto-feminist (see chapter eleven below). What boldness! He was a pioneer who dared to bring science into the heart of the Christian faith by way of a "pagan," and in doing so he angered the fundamentalists of his day. He insisted on the value of science to people of faith and all people: "All truth—whoever utters it—comes from the Holy Spirit." Nature, as well as the Bible, is a source of revelation. And always nature is sacred.

The boldness of Aquinas was well known in his time. He was so controversial that riots sometimes occurred at the convent where he was living due to parish priests arousing parishioners to confront him. He was condemned three times after his death. The "evangelical poverty" movement that the upstart Dominicans and Franciscans represented was a challenge to the monastic system that had married itself to the feudal system for centuries and was—surprise!— not eager to relinquish its power and privileges, whether in the fields of education, religion, or even architecture. I describe these realities (and much more) in the fifty-five page introduction to *Sheer Joy*, and I urge the reader to study that introduction to learn more of the times that shaped Aquinas and his amazing life story (one that truly deserves to be made into a movie for its drama and its importance). I also treat the "clay feet" of Aquinas, as I refuse to put our heroes on pedestals and insist on considering their shadows alongside their greatness.

One admiring student of Aquinas--a major poet of the beat generation, Bill Everson, known for sixteen years in the Dominican Order as Brother Antoninus, described the introduction to *Sheer Joy:* "Seizing Aquinas by scapular and capuche, Fox hands him point by point through the fundamental issues of our day. The introduction is the finest thing on Aquinas I have ever read. It picks him up where Pieper and Chenu left him in mid-century and lifts him boldly through the paradigm shift into the new millennium."

The Dalai Lama has remarked that the number one obstacle to interfaith relations is a bad relationship with one's own faith tradition. I would propose that Christians who do not know the deep, brilliant, passionate, and justice-oriented theology of Thomas Aquinas very likely do not know their own faith tradition. More and more I recognize that my job as an elder is to share that wisdom with the younger generation. I hope this short book opens up minds and hearts to the deeper meaning of the Christian lineage, that of the creation-spirituality tradition so fully incarnated by Thomas Aquinas.

When I was studying the history of Christian spirituality with the historian Louis Cognet at the

Institut Catholique de Paris I recall a lecture in which he asked the following question: "Why is there not one question in Aquinas's *Summa Theologiae* about spirituality? His answer was: "Because for Aquinas, everything is spiritual, spirituality is everywhere." And so it is.

Let us consider a brief summary of his life. Again, for much more, check out the introduction in *Sheer Joy*.

Thomas was born in 1225 in a castle named Roccasecca near Naples, Italy, of a family of lower nobility (his father, Landulf, was the count of Aquino) who knew early he was an exceptional child. They proceeded to place him in a Benedictine monastery at the age of five with high expectations that he might raise the family fortune by becoming abbot at Monte Cassino some day. But the sixteen-year-old Aquinas had other ideas. Having availed himself of a solid education for about ten years, he exited the Benedictine monastery and wandered to Naples where a new university (an invention of the late twelfth-century renaissance) had opened its doors in 1224.

There Aquinas encountered two exciting events that changed his life forever. First, he heard lectures by an Irish professor on Aristotle and science. The second was a new movement called the Dominican Order. Aquinas fell in love with both Aristotle and the Dominicans and joined the Order at nineteen years of age in Naples. But this was anathema to his family as the upstart Dominicans were considered far too avant-garde. As G. K. Chesterton put it, joining the Dominicans was tantamount to running away and marrying a gypsy.

What followed next was a drama worthy of a Hollywood story. His mother, now a widow, ordered his brothers to kidnap Thomas. They took him back to their castle where he was held in the dungeon for about a year. Eventually his sister liberated him, and he fled the area to join the Dominicans up north where he studied with the scientist-philosopher Albert the Great, first in Paris and then in Cologne. After ordination in Cologne he moved on to the University of Paris in 1252. A lecturer on scripture and on the *Sentences,* he was promoted to master of theology by a special papal dispensation because he was four years underage. Teaching theology in Paris from 1257 to 1259, he left for Italy and the papal court in Anagni, Orvieto, Rome, and Viterbo. In 1272 he returned to Paris to teach for three years, then continued on to teach in Naples. Throughout these years he wrote prolifically.

In December 1273, however, he underwent an experience that rendered him mute; he went silent and never wrote another word. The best guess is that he had a stroke that, like that of Fr. Bede Griffiths, doubled as a mystical breakthrough. He did manage to say that "such things have been revealed to me that all that I have written seems to me as so much straw." On March 7, 1274, he died in the Cistercian monastery of Fossanuova while journeying to Lyons for a church council. He was forty-nine years old.

Three years following his death, some of his teachings were condemned by the bishops of Paris and Canterbury. In 1323 he was canonized a saint. Current editions of his work fill twenty-five volumes averaging 650 encyclopedic-size pages with double columns. One scholar estimated that a compete edition of his works would fill forty to fifty volumes. No doubt he had a photographic memory. We are told that he kept four secretaries with him at a time to whom he dictated his thoughts. His books were written all within a twenty-one-year period (1252–73). I list them in *Sheer Joy*, but among them are commentaries on twelve of Aristotle's major works; many scriptural commentaries; the *Summa contra Gentiles* and *Summa Theologiae*, both major multivolume works; commentaries on Boethius and on Denys; and much more. A hint of the breadth and depth of his thinking can, I hope, be tasted in this current and brief volume.

I hope this book will prove to be a useful handbook

for spiritual activists and people looking for wisdom from our western lineage.

I have deliberately kept notes to a minimum because I do not want to clutter the text with notes. The references are all available in the mother tome to this book, *Sheer Joy: Conversation with Thomas Aquinas on Creation Spirituality*, which appeared first with HarperSanFrancisco, then with Jeremy P. Tarcher/Putnam, and—as of May 2020—from Dover Publications. I have devised a method of minimizing references by offering a single footnote to the *Sheer Joy* text on the first page of each chapter. Any subsequent references that are found within three pages of the original citation and appear within that chapter remain unmarked—the reader can simply go to the original text in *Sheer Joy*. At times within a paragraph I have also left notes unmarked that can be found in whatever page number is included within the paragraph.

The one exception to this method is chapter 27 (on angels) where the bulk of the references are to the book I coauthored with British scientist Rupert Sheldrake (who also wrote a foreword to *Sheer Joy*), *The Physics of Angels.* In that book Rupert and I dialogue with the teachings of Thomas Aquinas on angels (along with those of Denys the Areopagite and Hildegard of

Bingen), and the footnotes found there refer to Aquinas's discussions on angels.

I have tried here, as I did in *Sheer Joy*, to let Aquinas do the talking as much as possible. *Sheer Joy* provides a substantive and unique guide to Aquinas's thought as drawn from a uniquely broad spectrum of his writings. I divide our conversations in that book by way of the Four Paths of Via Positiva (Awe, Joy), Via Negativa (Silence, Grief, Letting Go), Via Creativa (Creativity) and Via Transformativa (Justice and Compassion), all of which are foundational to the tradition of creation spirituality. The book confirms without a doubt that this naming of the spiritual journey is deeply rooted in Aquinas's consciousness. Indeed, it was from his younger brother Meister Eckhart that I derived the Four Paths and first wrote about them.[3]

In an amazing passage in his Commentary on the Psalms Aquinas himself tells us that "the soul is elevated toward God in four ways." And he spells them out. First, "for the purpose of admiring the height of God's power, as Isaiah puts it: "Lift your eyes on high and see who creates these things" (Isa 40:36). Psalm 104 says: "How wonderful are your works, O Lord." Thus admiration and wonder—the Via Positiva—first sets our mind toward the divine.

Second, "the mind is raised for the purpose of

embracing the excellence of eternal beauty. Job 2 says: 'You can lift your face without stain, you will be able and you will not fear. You will also forget misery and a kind of noontime brightness will rise from you.' And this is the elevation of hope. The Via Negativa demands hope because both "misery" and "fear"' are experienced there. But a "noontime brightness" can sometimes break through the shadow, and contemplation assists that process.

Third, "the mind is raised to cling to divine good and sanctity, as Isaiah puts it: 'Awake, awake! Rise up, O Jerusalem' (51:17). And this is the elevation of charity." The Via Creativa is often a movement of waking up and rising up and being connected to the Holy Spirit, who creates goodness and charity.

Fourth, "the mind is raised to work for the imitation of divine justice. Lamentations 5 says: 'We will lift up our hearts with our hands to God in the heaven.' And this is the elevation of justice. The fourth way is also indicated when he says, 'To the holy and on high,' since the two last ways of elevation pertain to his saying, 'to the holy'; the first two ways pertain to when he says 'to you on high.'" (420) Clearly the Via Transformativa is being named here, for it is all about justice and compassion.

One reason for looking freshly at Aquinas today

is to ground the young who seek a deep spirituality leading to action. Aquinas offers such a substantive spiritual foundation. Another reason is to rediscover the profound influence Aquinas has had on numerous spiritual giants who drew directly from him: Mechtild of Magdeburg, Dante (Dante's primary teacher had been a student of Aquinas), Fr. Bede Griffith, Rupert Sheldrake, M.-D. Chenu, Yves Congar, Edward Schillebeeckx, Thomas Berry, Brian Swimme, and Teilhard de Chardin, to name a few. He was also a direct influence on his Dominican brother Meister Eckhart (who was seventeen years old when Aquinas died).

Intellectual history is very much a communal process—and since Aquinas profoundly influenced his younger Dominican brother, one would have to say that all subsequent thinkers who learned from Eckhart owe Aquinas a great debt. Anyone Eckhart influenced owes a serious debt of gratitude to Aquinas, for his influence is *indirect* by way of Eckhart. There would have been no Eckhart sans Aquinas.

Among those influenced by Eckhart directly—and hence by Aquinas *indirectly*—are: Carl Jung, Karl Marx, Thomas Merton, Martin Buber, Martin Heidegger, Howard Thurman, Julian of Norwich, John of the Cross, Teresa of Ávila, George Fox, the radical Protestants Hans Hutt, Sebastian Frank, and Hans Denk,

Dorothee Soelle, the author of the *Cloud of Unknowing,* the author of the *Theologia Germanica*, Martin Luther, Ignatius of Loyola, Peter Canisius, Paul of the Cross, John Tauler, Richard Hooker, Angelus Silesius, Jakob Boehme, Walter Hilton, Jan van Ruysbroeck, Howard Thurman, Martin Luther King Jr., Nicolas of Cusa, David Bohm, D. T. Suzuki, Ananda Coomeraswami, Rufus Jones, George Fox, G. W. F. Hegel, Rudolf Otto, Saul Bellow, John Updike, Annie Dillard, Alan Watts, Ira Progoff, Erich Fromm, and more.

It is quite a list, isn't it? You can see what a giant Aquinas was along with his famous pupil Meister Eckhart. Anyone grateful for any of these people above might necessarily be grateful to Aquinas—and likely curious and eager to know him firsthand.

Modern science itself may have been delayed in arriving if Aquinas had lacked the courage and intellectual imagination to (1) include the best science of his day (Aristotle as translated into Latin by Muslim scholars in Baghdad and Andalusia) and (2) employ the new "scholastic" pedagogy that arrived from Islam. Scholasticism in Aquinas's day represented a radical departure from patristic theology, since it was a method for asking and answering questions rather than simply citing long-dead authorities. In this way it helped open the door to modern science.

What has often been missed in Aquinas's work is how biblically based it is, how he began his teaching commenting on the scriptures, and how he wrote numerous commentaries on books of the Hebrew Bible and the Christian New Testament. In addition, his *Catena Aurea* is a major work (now in four volumes in English) that brings forth and arranges commentaries and sermons on the gospels by over eighty church fathers and provides a valuable resource for students of the Bible still today. His thought, while expansive scientifically and ecumenically, is profoundly grounded in the scriptures.

One might ask: What are you doing foisting medieval thinking onto twenty-first century problems? My answer is blunt: The modern era has specialized in knowledge, but no one can possibly argue that it has advanced in wisdom. In fact, as patriarchal and empire-oriented as it has been, it has banished the feminine, wisdom, and mysticism. So one goes to the missing and neglected parts of Western consciousness to attempt to balance our consciousness and redirect our civilization. And why settle for just minor or bit players? Why not invite the greatest minds and hearts into the dialog? Surely Aquinas is just such a person of substance.

Since this book draws on the primary sources that I share in *Sheer Joy*, I see this book as a kind of hors-d'oeuvre to that previous book, an appetizer or introduction to the deep questioning and seeking of truth that one finds everywhere in Aquinas. I have limited myself to thirty-one topics, as I think these represent pressing issues from our time upon which Aquinas sheds considerable wisdom. The reader is therefore encouraged to consult *Sheer Joy* for fuller development and a main course.

I have chosen my title, *The Tao of Thomas Aquinas* to underscore the wisdom for which he constantly strove, as wisdom is a favorite topic that Aquinas frequently invoked. It also hints at a convergence of east and west that is sorely needed today, as we strive to balance action with contemplation, and mysticism with the prophetic on a global scale. Consider this teaching from the *Tao Te Ching*:

> The Master concerns himself
> with the depths and not the surface,
> with the fruit and not the flower.
> He has no will of his own
> He dwells in reality
> And lets all illusions go.[4]

I see Aquinas in this passage with its emphasis on substance and on a mind free of illusions, and I recognize his teachings in numerous other teachings from the *Tao Te Ching.*

The link with the Tao is also a hint that east and west can cooperate today—as long as they operate out of the depths of their traditions and not at a superficial level.

My prayer is that all who read (and pray) this book will find themselves supported to participate generously in the bold, daring, fresh, discovery-filled, joy-and-justice-making adventure that Thomas Aquinas undertook and in which he delighted. Nothing less than a New Humanity and a New Earth are calling us.

The experience of God
must not be restricted
to the few
or to the old.

1. The experience of God must not be restricted to the few or to the old.*

Why does this observation from Aquinas excite me so much 800 years after they were spoken?

First, because *all spirituality leads with our experience of God.* In this book we are studying spirituality first. This is what distinguishes spirituality from religion—*spirituality is our experience of the divine.* Religion, on the other hand, is defined primarily today as a sociological category, a matter of buildings and numbers and money and hierarchy and institutional one-upmanship.

A number of years ago I was interviewed on Dutch television by an intelligent young man, and as soon as the show was over and the lights dimmed, he leaned over and said to me with a sense of urgency: "I have an important question for you that I have been wanting to ask for years."

"What is that?" I replied.

"Do you Americans still believe that people can experience God?"

He was correct. That *is* an important question. And the answer is Yes. At least some Americans are curious

---

* *Sheer Joy,* 1.

1

about and eager to experience the divine. We call that experience *spirituality.*

Notice how utterly nonelitist Aquinas is in his invitation—not the few and not the old hold a monopoly on experience of God. It is meant to be a democratic opportunity—one available to all. Because it is not exclusively for the old—the young are invited too, indeed they may be invited to lead. That seems to be happening today with leaders like Greta Thunberg addressing the climate emergency and high school students from Parkland, Florida, taking on the NRA.

I could say that my life's work as a spiritual theologian the past fifty-five years has been to uncover how we everyday folks experience the divine in our daily lives. One such way is through creation itself, as the poet Bill Everson attests: "Most people experience God in nature or experience God not at all." We are all called to be mystics (lovers) and prophets (people who stand up for justice) on a daily basis. What changes do we need to make, what transformations do we need to undergo, to taste the divine within and around us and how everyday can this be?

I am talking about *democratizing mysticism and its counterpart, prophecy,* and removing them from an elitist mindset that wants to restrict them to a few specialists (professional pray-ers, monks, or the equivalent). I believe we are all born mystics—that is, we all have minds and hearts that want to learn new things, get excited about life, taste awe and wonder, and build one's values around such profound experiences. Clearly, Aquinas was in this camp also—and centuries before "democracy" was a rallying cry. By insisting that *many* and not just a few are invited into experiencing the divine, he deconstructs the hierarchical thinking typical of both religion and society. He reinforces the beauty of all people, the intelligence of all people, the humanity of all people. We are all born for wonder and awe and stretching our souls.

He refuses to say that only the old know the divine. We all do. Children do. Teenagers and young adults do also. Challenging adultism in all its manifestations, Aquinas offers this interesting observation:

> Youth is the cause of hope on these three counts, namely, because the object of hope is future, is difficult, and is possible. For the young live in the future and not in the past; they are not lost in memories but full of confidence. Second, their warmth of nature, high spirits, and expansive heart embolden them to reach out to difficult projects; therefore they are mettlesome and of good hope. Third, they have not been thwarted in their plans, and their lack of experience

3

encourages them to think that where there's a
will there's a way. The last two factors, namely,
good spirits and a certain recklessness, are also
at work in people who are drunk." (349)

He also praises beauty found in the young. "For delight
is the perfection of happiness, as beauty is that of youth"
(505).

Yes, there is a certain optimism in being young, and
one profits from it by being around those who are. By
comparing the young to people who are drunk or high,
Aquinas highlights the importance of optimism, hope
and exuberance at living.

He encourages all to get a life—an *inner* life—
and start paying attention to our experiences of beauty
and truth, of oneness and oneing, in short to value our
mystical experiences and make them the basis of our
consciences, our choices, our values, our work, and
our goals. In many ways he is setting the stage for
his younger Dominican brother, Meister Eckhart, who
said that the person who is awake may experience
"breakthrough"—that is, our experience of God—
"not . . . once a year or once a month or once a day but
many times every day."[5]

Aquinas also echoes the wisdom scriptures such as
the psalms that say: "Taste and see that God is good"

(34:8). Tasting is something we all do—it is not done vicariously, nor is it done for us by some nobodaddy in the sky or some ordained prelate or pope. No one does it for us. We are responsible for learning life and drinking deeply from it. We can all taste the divine and thereby undergo the goodness of the divine. And of ourselves.

We taste the divine when we taste the wonder, the marvel, the surprise, the beauty, and the goodness of creation itself. And Aquinas develops this sense of the ecstatic on many occasions. He says, for example, that goodness and beauty go together, that they are distinguished only by the fact that beauty appeals more to the intellect than to the appetite.

He says that ecstasy is a sign of love and that we are all subject to it. He says that ecstasy and grace are not religious or profane, Christian or non-Christian, but that ecstasy is ecstasy and grace is grace.

He teaches that beauty is a way, a door, to the divine whether beauty be found in nature's sunsets or trees or animals or sky; or whether it be found in the human works of poetry and music and truth-seeking and truth-telling and work for justice and compassion.

Aquinas dismisses entirely the idea of a punitive father God or a God who only judges us (or teaches us to be overly judgmental). Rather, for him Divinity is a compassionate God, a God of love and a God of joy, who urges us to love and to develop virtues of compassion, justice, and love based on self-love. He encourages healthy self-love and wholesome pride when he insists: "Self-love is the form and root of all friendship. To know and appreciate your own worth is no sin" (99).

He teaches us to trust nature, to feel and love creation, to realize how thoroughly we are part of it and how much it has to teach us and how it awakens us and leads us to experiencing God. To trust nature we must trust ourselves, our own nature, and our own uniqueness--not to flinch at differences but to rejoice at diversity—at our being different and our being personally responsible for decisions we make while honoring differences in others.

In opting for an ethic of virtue over an ethic of obedience to rules, he forcibly resists the childish mentality of catechisms that set us up with binary questions and answers about morality that pave the way for burdensome guilt and shame. He also stands up to fascist mentalities that rely on the powerful or the few to tell others what is good and bad and who consider obedience a greater virtue than creativity or compassion or developing a conscience.

Aquinas tells us that when a truly important ethical question arises, one will not find the answer in a book, but rather should seek counsel from a mature, ethical person—and then make your own determination about right and wrong. He therefore urges the development of conscience.

In declaring that "the experience of God should not be restricted to the few or to the old," Aquinas celebrates the existence, the wisdom, and the potential maturity of every human being. None are excluded from this school of wisdom, this pilgrimage of growth, this growing of a soul that life invites us to undergo.

I have intentionally offered this first saying as our kickoff point, because this book is primarily about our experience of the divine—and my goal is for younger readers to awaken to that experience. After all, this is what spirituality is about, and it is important to begin with the many blessings—indeed the *original blessings*—that have called us into existence. Another term for that original blessing is *the cosmos.* It birthed us after all. We did not birth it.

We are all in it, and it is in all of us. It is not only good but *very good.* The universe is the starting point of our existence, of the air we breathe and the water we drink and the food we eat and those of the songs we sing and dance to and the joys of our lives. We are in it and it is in us. It is the kingdom of God.

"They shall be drunk
with the beauty of thy house,"
that is,
the universe.

2. 'They shall be drunk with the beauty of thy house,' that is, the Universe.*

The psalmist invites us to ecstasy and inebriation on the beauty of God's house. But Aquinas explains the origin of our spiritual intoxication with one word: *the universe*. Yes, the universe exists to get us drunk. The universe exists to make us joyful beyond measure. The universe does not just *exist*, however—it has acted for this very reason: it has brought *us* into existence. It invites us to inebriation. Rabbi Heschel declares that the universe "shocks us into amazement"—indeed, a radical amazement.

Aquinas proposes that being drunk means our "desires will be filled beyond all measurement of merit. For intoxication is a kind of excess, as the Song of Songs says, 'my beloved, you are drunk with love'" (110). Love of the universe renders us drunk. The many new discoveries of the universe by science in our time has increased the occasions for such drunkenness. Ecstasy is another term for being drunk for "those who are drunk are not inside of themselves but outside of themselves" (109).

Aquinas had only a general view of evolution insofar as he insists that God did not just make creation

---

* *Sheer Joy*, 124.

9

and walk away but that creation is still going on. "God's work whereby God brings things into being must not be taken as the work of a craftsman who makes a box and then leaves it. For God continues to give being." (125)

Of course, Aquinas did not know what we know about evolution and the universe today. He did not know that the universe is 13.8 billion years in the making and continues to give birth and expand. He did not know that the universe possesses *two trillion galaxies*, each with hundreds of billions of stars—so many, in fact, that there are more stars in the universe than there are grains of sand on all the beaches of the earth!

No, Aquinas did not have all of today's facts about the universe in front of him. Although, for that matter, neither did Newton or Einstein, for science is always expanding our knowledge. Nor did Aquinas have a sufficiently historic consciousness with a sense of evolution in the entire context of existence as we know it today. Consider this consciousness in light of our new creation story—the one that begins with an original pinprick of darkness that erupts into a fireball. Says Aquinas: "In the first days God created all things in their origins or causes. . . . Afterward, by governing the creatures, in the work of propagation, 'God works until now'" (129).

But Aquinas did know one very important dimension

to the universe that we modern and postmodern peoples have easily forgotten—namely, that the facts of our home, the universe, are only part of the story. The other part is our response to that existence—our excitement, awe, wonder, and gratitude. We have a right to get drunk on existence itself, on the realization that we, contrary to all odds, exist at all. As Heschel puts it, "the existence of the world is the most unlikely, the most unbelievable fact. . . . the existence of the universe is contrary to all reasonable expectations."[6] Or consider Eckhart: "Isness is God." The isness of the universe has birthed our existence and made it possible. And existence anywhere, isness anywhere, is godly.

Knowledge is not enough. Facts are not enough. The poet Mary Oliver exclaims, "I want to be dazzled." Being dazzled is about being drunk, inebriated, out of the box of the rational and the factual, being touched at a deep place of wonder and awe.

What is awe? This is how Rabbi Heschel, who derives from the same spiritual tradition as Jesus, talks about it. Awe "enables us to perceive in the world intimations of the divine. . . . What we cannot comprehend by analysis we become aware of in awe."[7] No wonder "awe is the beginning of wisdom." Aquinas also links awe and wisdom. "One meditates on creation in order to view and marvel at divine wisdom. . . .

Indeed, divine wisdom first appears in the creation of things." Both the poet and the philosopher begin with "amazement" for "wonder causes inquiry" (78, 101).

Universe means oneness. Mysticism is also about oneness or "oneing" with God, as Julian of Norwich puts it. Maybe this is why Einstein said that for him "this oneness of creation is God."[8] Both Judaism and Islam celebrate how "God is one" at the center of their prayer.

In celebrating the ecstasy we undergo vis-à-vis the universe, Aquinas is also talking about ecology. Why is that so? Thomas Berry, eco-prophet and self-styled geologian, teaches that "ecology is functional cosmology." Furthermore, *eco* is the Greek word for "home"—and Aquinas states explicitly that the cosmos and creation are our home and God's home. Are we at home in the universe? In the cosmos? Are we stepping back from our computers or our shopping trips often enough to look into our home, the universe, to study it? Or have we succumbed completely to the disastrous modern era that began with the divorce of science and spirituality, cosmos and psyche?

In calling us back to the wonder, beauty, and ecstasy of the universe, Aquinas offers us profound medicine and healing for the rupture of psyche and spirit that haunts modern men and women and opens the door to anthropocentrism, to forgetfulness and destruction of the planet, and to what Pope Francis has rightly called our narcissism as a species. We are being called back to the premodern consciousness found among indigenous peoples everywhere, but also among medieval thinkers such as Hildegard of Bingen, Francis of Assisi, and Thomas Aquinas, who did not put humans on a pedestal but imagined us properly within the entire web of life.

In Aquinas's language, as in today's science, the web of life is called *interconnectivity*. "That all things are related to each other is evident from the fact that all are interconnected together to one end," he observes. "The perfection of any one thing considered in isolation is an imperfection, for one thing is merely one part of the entire integrity of the universe arising from the assembling together of many singular perfections." This is not modern individualism being preached. Community, the kinship of all beings that make up one beautiful whole, the cosmos is at stake. Moreover, "All things are connected in a common bond of friendship with all nature"—indeed, all things in the universe "seek God and desire God" with whom they share a common "friendship" (90–93).

For Aquinas, the universe is our house, our home. Who would despoil or destroy one's own home? There is something intimate about home and our relationship to it. Intimacy is part of grandeur, it is part of our mystical lives wherein we are connected to something bigger than ourselves—not in a superficial way but deeply, in a way that gives us life and meaning and purpose. The universe does all that for us—it brought us into being along with all the other creatures that are necessary for our existence: the sun and moon, the earth and water, the plants and animals, the trees and forests, the soil and ozone. Yes, we are truly interdependent beings. That is what a human being is. And there is intimacy—in Aquinas's words, friendship—in all of these relationships. One is reminded of the most sacred prayer of the Lakota people—"all our relations"—they are all sacred, they are all to be acknowledged and thanked and praised.

And they all render us drunk, outside of ourselves, and therefore ecstatic. Aquinas tells us that "love and also zeal are caused in us from beauty and goodness." Objects of zeal are "intensely lovable" (114–15). Beauty is our medicine—falling in love with earth and her creatures, with the universe, our true home—there lies the medicine for waking us all up to love of life and combatting the forces within and without us that are killing the earth.

Of course to speak of "getting drunk" on God's house or the universe is a special way of talking about what the mystics call the Via Positiva, that experience of the deep-down beauty of existence, of our planet, of being alive, of love of life in spite of all its demands and challenges. It is about generating a gratitude and reverence that emerge from awe and wonder. It is well summarized in Meister Eckhart's simple words: "If the only prayer you say in your whole life is 'Thank you,' that would suffice."

Clearly, Thomas Aquinas is in every way a mystic and champion of the Via Positiva. He invites us to be the same. And it all begins with an astonishing and ecstatic experience that we call the universe.

**Revelation comes
in two volumes:
Nature
and the Bible**

3. Revelation comes in two volumes: Nature and the Bible.*

Aquinas insists that all people should study nature and that our meditation on nature opens up the divine to us. "One meditates on creation in order to view and marvel at divine wisdom" (78). Citing the psalmist who sings, "I meditate on all your works, I muse on the work of your hands" (Ps 143:5), Aquinas comments: "Meditation is indispensable for well-instructed faith." And since "all creatures confess that they are made by God," it is our job as humans to examine creatures for the revelation of the divine that they carry within them (80–81).

If all things are "God's works of art," then to examine the art is to get to know the Artist. He tells us this: "Jesus teaches us to avoid anxiety by considering the birds of the sky, since there is wisdom from them. Also in Job we read, 'Ask the cattle and they will teach you' (Job 12:7)." All of creation is eager to reveal the divine mystery and so it follows that "there can be no question that to study creatures is to build up one's Christian faith." To run from science or to put science down is an affront to authentic faith because "the opinion is false of those who assert that it makes no difference to the truth of the faith what anyone holds about creatures, so long as one thinks

---

* *Sheer Joy,* 59.

rightly about God. For error about creatures spills over into false opinion about God, and take peoples' minds away from God, to whom faith seeks to lead them" (75).

Thus it is little wonder that Aquinas tells us that "sacred writings are bound in two volumes—that of creation and that of the Holy Scriptures." It is stunning, given the fundamentalism and bibliolatry of so much of what passes as Christianity today— with its own television and radio station conglomerates and well-financed marriages of religion and politics—to hear these powerful words from a brilliant thirteenth-century theologian who says bluntly: *The Bible is not enough!*

And never has it been. We must study nature too for a profound witness; revelation to the divine lies there as well as in written scriptures. Of course the study of nature today is different from Thomas's day insofar as we know so much more about the cosmos.

Were Aquinas alive today, there is no question that he would be head over heels with excitement to learn the marvels that science has revealed for us. He would be beside himself with the news of the 13.8 billion years it has taken to birth our world and the size of the universe in which we find ourselves. He would, in his own words, *marvel* at all these marvels. Or, shall we say, "get drunk with the plenty of thy house," as we saw in the second chapter.

It is telling, for example, that the word "Lord" for Aquinas does not mean "lord and savior." No, "Lord" for Aquinas is a cosmic title. He says: "The word 'Lord' means the maker of all creation. As in Judith 16: 'All your creation serves you.'" The word "God" for Aquinas is not about "God and us" but about all of creation. "The word 'God' signifies the governor and provider of all things. To believe there is a God is to believe in one whose government and providence extend to all things." His very definition of God extends to and embraces all of creation. He never wanders far from the sacredness of creation. And, of course, the word and work of God suggest classic concepts of the *logos* and the Cosmic Christ. "In the beginning was the Word (*logos*)" (John 1:1).

We turn to creatures to learn God for good reason for "visible creatures are like a book in which we read the knowledge of God. One has every right to call God's creatures God's 'words,' for they express the divine mind just as effects manifest their cause. 'The works of the Lord are the words of the Lord' (Eccl 42:15)." We are to read creatures as we do books. Creatures can therefore be objects of the practice of *lectio divina*—and they ought to be. We contemplate them just as monks contemplate the biblical scriptures. Both are spiritual practices to awaken and strengthen the soul.

The greatness of the human person
consists in this:
that we are
capable of the universe.

4. The greatness of the human person consists in this: that we are capable of the universe.[*]

The proof that Aquinas is a premodern thinker who has much in common with indigenous wisdom is that he celebrates, first and foremost, our relationship to the cosmos, which, as we have seen, elicits ecstasy and drunkenness. Indeed, that cosmos is more excellent than human beings. "God has produced a work in which the likeness of God is clearly reflected—that is, the world itself" (158). Our greatness as a species he declares, is that we are "*capax universi*, capable of the universe."

What an eye-opener and game-changer this is! Aquinas is urging humans to get beyond our own hurts and wounds and petty agendas and look at the big picture. He recognized that the universe is our mother and, therefore, ought not be neglected in the way we look at the world.

Our bigness of mind, our vastness of intellect and imagination, all urge us to look out into a world so much larger than ourselves. It is not enough to live in the worlds we make. We must consider *the world that makes us.* He invites us to welcome cosmology and those who study it! And to grow our souls. With the growing of our souls there comes more courage

---

[*] *Sheer Joy*, 138.

(*grand coeur*, or "big heart" in French), more creativity, more joy.

Aquinas marvels that we are capable of such a reach at all. "Other beings take only a limited part in being. But the spiritual being is capable of grasping the whole of being" and "embracing the whole of being." He speaks of our vast capacity to know and understand this way: "There is nothing that the human mind cannot understand potentially. It is capable of knowing all things."

In terms of our creativity he says: "Instead of the knowledge and power in regard to fixed and particular things, human beings have by nature their reason and their hands." What we can accomplish with our hands and our reason is vast for "by these means human beings can make for themselves instruments of an *infinite variety* and for any number of purposes." Isn't it true that no two musicians have composed the same song? Or two painters painted the same painting? Or any two poets composed the same poems? Does this not imply that our creativity is infinite?

He elaborates on our immense intellectual capacities when he says that we have "a power extending to the infinite." And our "intellectual natures have a closer relationship to a whole than do other natures." We "may comprehend the entirety of being through our intellect" and "our intellect never understands so many things that it could not understand more." Aquinas is talking about what we today call *consciousness*: "There is something that relates to the totality of existing things. The soul is such a being that, as is said in [Aristotle's] *The Soul,* 'in some way is all things'" (142).

A mistake about creation
results in
a mistake about God.

5. A mistake about creation results in a mistake about God.*

It is difficult to come across any statement that more deeply celebrates the vocation of the scientist's search for truth than this one from Thomas Aquinas: That "a mistake about creation results in a mistake about God."

All the mistakes we make about nature steer us away from our understanding of Divinity. Consider the mistake that says homosexuality is "contrary to nature" (which it may be for heterosexuals but not for homosexuals, who constitute roughly 8 percent of any human population). Furthermore we have counted 464 other species that sport homosexual populations. Or the mistake that the difference between races is anything but a superficial difference. Or the mistake that we live on a flat earth, or on an earth around which the sun turns, or that stars are eternal; or that species have always been here, or that the earth is 6500 years old, or that God punishes us through disease, or that men are active and women are passive, or that men are born to rule, or that there has always been patriarchy, and so on. Yes, "a mistake about creation results in a mistake about God."

Aquinas's observation underscores the value and

---

* *Sheer Joy*, 22.

necessity of our searching for truth. "Only the truth will make you free," *and* only the truth will result in fewer mistakes about God. Of which humans can cling to very many indeed.

Among other examples, one can point to the mistake that God is homophobic, or misogynist, or racist, or in love with empires and empire-building, or an old white man in the sky or restricted to the sky "out there" at all, or on the side of the powerful, or a punitive father, or a judge and ethereal peeping tom who cares exclusively about our sex lives, or a thruster into hell and eternal damnation and hellfire, or sadistic, or made in the image of man, or out to get us, or believer in original sin, or angry all the time, or a shame dispenser, or a bestower of guilt, or one who hates us. In fact, Aquinas insists: "God cannot hate anything." (119)

Humans regularly project onto Divinity our own unexamined shadows, and this renders Divinity often very scary indeed.

But let us flip this saying around. If a mistake about creation results in a mistake about God, isn't it true also that an insight about creation might result in an insight about God? For example, that absorbing the truths of evolution gives us an insight into the way Divinity operates, with patience and with lots of coming and going, living and dying, resurrecting and spreading seeds of new life. Species come and go, stars come and go and resurrect, galaxies and supernovas come and go and resurrect. Creativity and birthing are at the heart of the habits of the universe—indeed the cosmos exhibits habits that we call the paschal mystery of life, death, and resurrection. We find these played out with stars, galaxies, and supernovas. Or the truth that relationship lies at the heart of things. And that things are not just things but relationships. That emptiness is a big part of an atom and of a galaxy. That darkness and mystery such as Dark Energy and Dark Matter play significant roles in the universe. And do our psyches also reflect a psychic version of dark energy and dark matter, of shadow and potential for evil?

Other truths inform us that all things have a shadow, the human species very much included and that good habits are necessary to lessen the shadow's influence on us. Truths that interdependence is everywhere and where there is interdependence compassion is possible because compassion is the working out of our interdependence. Truths that art and symbol and metaphor and myth and ritual are part of all human tribes because we all seek to praise and share and remember our deep experiences of both joy and sorrow that touch our hearts and call forth our common humanity and common dreams and needed healing. That the body is an amazing gift and deserves to be cared for and understood and wondered at (see chapter 11). That plants and animals, soil and forests, oceans, rivers and fishes all have their stories to tell as well as their beauty to share.

But the painful truths of nature also need revealing. For example, climate change *is* happening and the implications of this for the future of the human race and so many other species. Glaciers *are* melting, and seas *are* rising, droughts and firestorms are multiplying, and floods are increasing, storms and hurricanes are becoming more frequent and devastating (and, consequently, migrations will increase), the acidity of the oceans is increasing, and species are disappearing at an alarming rate, from insects to polar bears, from tigers to trees, from plants to fishes. Science warns us—as an ancient prophet—of the bad news as well as the good. All this offers insight about the divine and what it asks of us today.

Aquinas's observation about truth and our understanding of God elevates the scientific vocation, since scientists are in pursuit of the truths behind and within nature. He almost baptizes scientists as priests or "midwives of grace" (my definition of the priestly archetype). After all, scientists explore the grace of truth-finding, truth discovery, truth-telling, and truth-sharing even when it may be an inconvenient truth or an uncomfortable one.[9] We are made aware of our current climate emergency—and, hopefully, some solutions to it—by scientific observation and truth-telling.

Aquinas insists that our knowledge of God is relative to our knowledge about creation and nature—including human nature. Nor is this just armchair speculation from him. After all, he devoted his whole life to bringing science into religion in spite of fierce opposition. He devoted himself to synthesizing his religious beliefs with Aristotle, whose "discovery" and translations by Islamic scholars were the newest intellectual revolution of the times in Europe. But Aristotle arrived with three strikes against him:

1. He was a scientist—fundamentalists in Aquinas's day (like those in our own) were not interested in science, since they felt all truth was contained within the Bible.
2. He was a "pagan."
3. He came by way of Islam.

Aquinas also brought the new methodology of Islamic scholasticism into Christian places of learning. Scholasticism was a revolution in itself because it threw out the traditional monastic teaching by way of citing old, dead patriarchs and substituted it with asking questions and seeking objective answers. Scholasticism therefore was a prelude to modern science. Aquinas himself, then, was a prelude to modern science in many ways.

For all these reasons, Aquinas was very controversial in his day. Stories are told that the French king had to call out his troops at times to surround the convent where Aquinas lived because local priests had so encouraged their parishioners to attack him at home— all because he dared to bring a pagan scientist into the faith. Courage, then, was part of Aquinas's love of truth and his commitment to science.

"Love of God presupposes knowledge of God," declares Aquinas (181). Thus science is a door that leads us to love God more fully. Knowledge matters—and, therefore, science matters.

Sheer Joy is God's
and this demands
companionship.

6. Sheer Joy is God's, and this demands companionship.*

On the lips of many scientists of our day there lies these questions: What is the purpose of the universe? Why does it exist? And why do we exist? We have in this one sentence Aquinas's answer to these questions: "Sheer Joy is God's, and this demands companionship."

Aquinas proposes that the universe exists for the sake of Joy—God's and that of the rest of us. "All beings are gladly doing their best to express God," says Meister Eckhart. In our own time, geologian and eco-prophet Thomas Berry, who was not only named after Thomas Aquinas but admired him and quoted him often, offered his own take on this teaching when he declared: "In the end the universe can only be explained in terms of celebration. It is all an exuberant expression of existence itself."[10] Berry carried Aquinas's sense of joy into the twenty-first century for us.

Is celebration at the heart of existence? Is existence inherently joyful? Of course there are struggles and hardships. But why dwell on that when the real surprise, the real gift, is that we exist at all (and that it's taken 13.8 billion years of work on the universe's part to bring us here and sustain us). Even stars, supernovas, and

* *Sheer Joy,* 100.

33

galaxies live, die, and resurrect—why should humans be exempt? Or the other animals and plants and all? The issue is not whether there is suffering in life, but whether life is a joy *in spite of* the suffering. Do we make room for the Via Positiva and the joy it names? Can we maintain the joy amidst the pain?

The human species—unlike any other species—often chooses to dwell in self-pity rather than getting on to the task of sustainability and survival so that we all survive and flourish as partners in a joint celebration of existence.

In spite of the struggle toward survival of the fittest, can joy reign? It is a big question to which Aquinas offers a clear and blunt answer. He attributes the existence of the universe not only to joy but also to the inherent desire within joy to be shared with others. Joy begs for sharing. Who wants to be joyful all alone? Isn't joy naturally oriented to expansion, including others and sharing the joy? That is what Aquinas proposes. The greatest of joy, that of divinity itself, seeks to share the joy and not to hoard it. Fear restricts; but Joy expands and seeks companions with whom to share itself.

"God delights. God is always rejoicing and doing so with a single and simple delight. In fact, it is appropriate to say that love and joy are the only human emotions that we can attribute literally to God" (118). Aquinas is a long way from a punitive father God.

It follows that for Aquinas Joy is at the heart of the universe—what else would follow from the teaching of the original goodness, or original blessing? After all, goodness renders us joyful. We seek its company, we want it around, and we smile in its presence. Aquinas returns to this theme of the presence of joy on many occasions. For example, he says that "God is supremely joyful and therefore supremely conscious." Notice how he links joy and consciousness. Isn't it true that you feel most alive when you are most joyful? Isn't that what joy does to us? Aquinas attributes the consciousness of Divinity to the amount of joy that Divinity carries.

Is this also true of us? Are we most conscious when we are most joyful? Is that when we see the world in all its brightness and splendor? Do consciousness and joy play off of each other? Consider its opposite. Is sadness a kind of darkness that snuffs out joy and render us less alive, less conscious? No wonder we are, in our depths, such blessed and joyful beings.

**Joy
is the human's
noblest act.**

7. Joy is the human's noblest act.[*]

That "joy is the human's noblest act" might amaze us. Really? Is Joy our noblest act? Why not fighting for justice or dying for a noble cause? Aquinas reminds us that even justice exists for the sake of joy—a just world is a balanced world and is therefore conducive to joy for the many, not just the few. Justice is not an end in itself, but joy is. To remain in joy through hardship and loss, disappointment and struggle, is no small thing. It demands a deep spiritual life. A depth of soul. Working for justice in order to share the joy, renders joy more available to more people.

Furthermore, joy is part of compassion. As Eckhart, faithful disciple of Aquinas that he was, put it: "What happens to another whether it be a joy or a sorrow happens to me." Eckhart is defining what compassion is—it is, on the one hand, a celebration of our common joy; on the other hand, however, it is an acknowledgment of our common suffering as we fight the good fight for healing and justice (so that joy can return). As we have seen, it is the playing out of our interdependence.

Both Eckhart and Aquinas say that "God is compassion." It follows that to become compassionate is

---

* *Sheer Joy*, 120.

godlike, as Jesus noted: "Be you compassionate as your Creator in heaven is compassionate" (Luke 6:36). Thus joy and compassion are indeed our noblest acts—our most godlike acts.

Might this change everything? The way we do education? Politics? Religion? Economics? Art? What would happen if we built a civilization on joy? What values would change?

Who is leading this "noblest of acts"? Who is showing us the paths to get there?

Aquinas teaches that "love is the cause of joy," and he offers proof: "Everyone takes joy in their beloved," and "love and joy constitute the basis of all attraction—love is the origin and joy is the end result" (118, 433). Thus love and joy go together, so both love and joy constitute our noblest acts. Aquinas reminds us that "the only person who truly has joy is one who lives in love" (116). The consciousness of God is about love and joy, and the same is true of human consciousness. A call to love is a call to joy. And a call to joy is a call to love and sharing that love.

**Religion is
supreme thankfulness
or gratitude**

8. Religion is supreme thankfulness or gratitude.[*]

It is striking how Aquinas understands (and does not understand) religion. He claims that "it is evident that religion is a virtue," and of course a virtue is an inner habit in a person that empowers as one repeatedly practices it. Notice what Aquinas is *not* saying, however. He is not putting religion into a sociological category; he is silent about buildings and structures, institutions, rules, and lists of moral dos and don'ts. These do not constitute the essence of religion.

But what is this virtue all about that we call religion? Says Aquinas: "Religion is supreme thankfulness or gratitude." It is essentially about the goodness and blessing we have inherited and our grateful response. It is primarily about the Via Positiva. Where does this gratitude derive from? "The debt of gratitude flows from charity" says Aquinas. A certain reverence derives from the acknowledgment of the goodness of our existence and all that makes that possible by way of the goodness of all creatures. It is religion's task to make that reverence live. "It belongs to religion to show reverence to One God under a single aspect, namely, as the first principle of the creation and government of things."

---

[*] *Sheer Joy*, 359.

Notice he is not saying that religion is primarily about redemption—rather it is primarily about gratitude and reverence. Thankfulness is not coerced, and neither is true religion. "Gratitude is paid spontaneously. Thanking is less thankful when it is compelled."

It follows that religion is primarily a matter of the heart, for "gratitude depends chiefly on the heart." The primary purpose of the sabbath, as we are told in scripture, is to give thanks *for creation*. The "seventh day" described in Genesis implies that the command to "remember to keep holy the sabbath day" is about giving thanks.

But religion is not any gratitude—it is a *supreme gratitude* according to Aquinas. What makes it so "supreme"? Is it that we have an ultimate act of gratitude to give the Creator? Is this the bottom line for gratitude—our existence? And gratitude therefore for so many other beings that are beautiful in their own right and also necessary for our survival? Within Aquinas's teaching about gratitude we can see the origins of Meister Eckhart's teaching that "if the only prayer you say in your whole life is 'Thank You' that would suffice."

What is the opposite of gratitude? Taking something for granted. Forgetfulness. Taking and not giving back. Receiving and refusing to give or give back. Taking but not returning blessing for blessing and goodness for goodness. Aquinas actually talks about the church as "a garden," again resisting the image of a religious institution in favor of a plot of the good earth, a source from which there flows sustenance, beauty, and nourishment.

The first and primary
meaning of salvation is this:
To preserve things
in the good.

9. The first and primary meaning of salvation is this: To preserve things in the good.[*]

Having lived seventy-nine years on this planet, and having heard quite a few sermons and religious teachers over the years, I remain quite nervous whenever I hear the words "salvation" or "redemption." Perhaps that is because history reminds us that those who are busy "saving" or "redeeming" others are often rather shortsighted regarding their own limitations and those of the ideologies to which they adhere. I am thinking of crusades and inquisitions, of witch burnings and book burnings, of declarations of heresy and all the rest—dark forces of projections and scapegoating done in the name of a punitive deity wrapped in the clothing of orthodoxy and power. The term "lord and savior Jesus Christ," for example, often makes my hair stand on end—savior of what? Of whom? From what? From where? For what end?

It is so rare, therefore, to hear words like those of Aquinas at the start of this chapter. He gives us his definition of salvation—good! That is so needed if we dare use the word at all, for it is, as I indicated above, so easily misused and abused in the name of a punitive deity. Not only does he provide a meaning of

---

[*] *Sheer Joy*, 32.

"salvation," but he insists that his meaning is both "first" and "primary." A double first! "Salvation squared," we might call it.

And what does he come up with? Salvation, first and foremost, means: "To preserve things in the good."

Isn't that stunning? Notice what he is *not* saying. He is not saying anything about saving us from hell or even getting to heaven, a place beyond this place we call earth or a time beyond our lifetimes. Nor is he even talking about humans in particular. He is talking about *things*—about all things, about beings, about creation, about the cosmos, about the earth, about the elephants and giraffes, the rainforests and the oceans, the fishes and the soil, the trees and the birds and, yes, humans. He is applying the theme of cosmic awareness that we discussed in a previous chapter.

And he is also talking—still again—of *goodness.* Goodness preoccupies Aquinas. Goodness comes first. It is always on his mind; he sees it everywhere. He says God is "sheer goodness." And again he applies goodness too to the entire cosmos when he says: "All things are good because they flow from the fount of goodness. We can praise God through all things!" God is the fount of goodness, therefore, who bestows the "infinite goodness on each creature according to its unique capacity." Think of it! Goodness is everywhere, every being is bearing goodness. "Every being as being is good," he insists. We live in, breathe in, and swim in a world of goodness.

Furthermore, in Aquinas's worldview the universe is not only good—it is *very good.* Commenting on the creation story presented in the first page of the Bible, he writes: "In the Book of Genesis it says, 'God saw all things that God had made, and they were very good, each one of them having been previously said to be good. For each thing in its nature is good, but all things together are very good, by reason of the order of the universe, which is the ultimate and noblest perfection in things'" (98). Here again he is celebrating the interconnectivity of all things. But he also names the "ultimate and noblest" perfection in things as their relationship to the overall order of the universe.

Taking on the temptations of anthropocentrism and narcissism head on, he declares that "it is false to say that humanity is the most excellent being in the world" (89). The universe is the most excellent thing! "God wills that human beings exist for the sake of the perfection [or coming to maturity or wholeness] of the universe" (93). Once again, Aquinas is high on existence, high on all the parts of creation, but the creation itself as a whole is the "most excellent thing of all."

"All nature is good. . . . All things are good because

they flow from the fount of goodness. We can praise God through all things!" Furthermore, "nature is related to blessedness as first is related to second. Blessedness is grounded on nature. There is no thing that does not share in goodness and beauty" (96). What a cure for patriarchal cynicism lies in these words!

To praise and sing and celebrate the goodness in things and in the whole is the very starting point of Aquinas's theology. There is another theological word for *goodness* and that is *blessing.* What is blessing? He says: "To bless is nothing else than to *speak the good.* In one way we bless God and in another way God blesses us. We bless God by recognizing the divine goodness." Notice what he is saying: to adhere to original blessing, to see our lives and home—the universe—as original blessing, and our earth and its bountiful creatures is how "*we bless God.*" He tells us that the "Holy Spirit proceeds as the love of the *primal goodness* whereby the Creator loves the Godhead and every creature" (159). The term "primal goodness" sounds an awful lot like "original blessing" to me. As do his terms "original goodness" and "original freshness" (100).

Our blessing God is an act of returning goodness for goodness, blessing for blessing, to recognize goodness all around us (and within us). This seems to be very much a statement about the "kingdom/queendom of

God" of which Jesus spoke so often. It is all around us and among us and within us—and of course it is very good, and it is blessing. We bless God by acknowledging this. It is creation.

But Aquinas adds another point when he adds: "And God blesses us by causing goodness in us." Once more, notice what he is *not* saying. He is not saying that God blesses us by giving us things or answering our prayers or by intervening miraculously in the midst of our woes. No. God blesses us "by causing goodness in us." God blesses us by causing blessing in us, by beautifying us from the inside, by rendering us good on the inside just as the rest of creation is good. Goodness is not an outside thing—it is an inner thing. Blessing is that way too.

Aquinas gifts us with a profound theology of *original blessing.* For the universe is original, it alone houses our origins, and it is the "most excellent thing of all," the ultimate in goodness or blessing.[11]

Now we can more fully grasp Aquinas's understanding of salvation, a meaning of salvation that is perfectly fitted for a time like ours when the goodness of creation is in jeopardy. Just today, as I write these words, there are fires raging here in northern California. Over 75,000 acres have already burned up, and hundreds of homes and businesses have been destroyed. The skies are grey and the air toxic—so toxic that I wonder if I dare take my dog for a walk for concern that she could be harmed by inhaling the fumes of smoke and fire. What a contrast to the blue skies and greenery for which northern California is so famous!

Here we move from blessing and goodness to curse and toxins—*that* is what climate change is bringing about. All creatures are suffering from it, including many parents whose children cannot go to school, business owners who have to abandon their stores, workers of all kinds who are prevented from getting to work.

We live in a world now that can no longer take health for granted. Or blue skies, for that matter. Or green lands, pure air, or clean water. We are losing goodness, losing blessing, because we have taken so much for granted for so long and thereby concluded that we can treat the land however we like.

It is in this context that Aquinas's definition of salvation shouts out to us: "To preserve things in the good." Can we do that? Are we up to it? How do we do that? What resources of intelligence and creativity must we muster to preserve the goodness of this planet? That is a question for all scientists and engineers, healers and politicians, educators and lawyers, ministers, priests, rabbis, and imans, artists and filmmakers—indeed, all citizens must answer. We share this understanding of salvation in common: *Preserving things in the good is the name of the game today.* We are not making things good. Nature has done that. Creation and Creator have done that. We are here to keep that good going, to preserve things in the good. All hands on deck! This is why we are all called to be at this common work, a salvific work, together—to preserve things in the good, in their state of original blessing.

It is our invitation to pass on the goodness to future generations not yet born. To "preserve things in the good" is to preserve them in their original blessing. Thomas Berry calls this "the great work."[12]

Finally, notice that in this "first and primary" meaning of salvation there is no word about (1) avoiding hell; (2) getting to heaven after this life; (3) curing an original sin; (4) obeying all the rules; or (5) pleasing a punitive father God. The whole context for religion is flipped when one begins with original blessing—as Aquinas does in this teaching. He is calling us to our responsibility as participants in the community we call earth and our home, the universe. He therefore gives us an eco-theology (since "eco" means home).

The same Spirit
who hovered over the waters
at the beginning of creation
hovers over the mind of the artist at work.

10. The same Spirit who hovered over the waters at the beginning of creation hovers over the mind of the artist at work.[*]

Aquinas had a lot to say about God as artist—and by extension about us, born in God's image and likeness—as artists. Regarding the former, he used the term "artist" about God perhaps more than any other single name. For example, he declares that "God is an artist and the universe is God's work of art." And again, "all natural things are produced by divine art and can rightly be called God's work of art" (65). God is "the Artist of artists."

How does it feel to be called "God's work of art"? Compare it, for example, to being called a "sinner," a "wretch," a "worm," or an object of judgment and wrath by a punitive father God in the sky.

Aquinas draws an important conclusion from his premise that nature is God's work of art when he says: "All artists love what they give birth to—parents love their children; poets love their poems; craftspeople love their handiwork. How then could God hate a single thing since God is the artist of everything?" (66) God takes delight in us just as the artist takes delight in his or her paintings, poetry, writing, dance, pottery, filmmaking, and playwriting. There is a love relationship between

---

[*] *Sheer Joy*, 248.

God and nature (including humans, who are so integral to nature). This echoes, of course, Hildegard of Bingen's erotic teaching that God and creation are related as lovers.

Aquinas says: "God's spirit is said to move over the waters as the will of the artist moves over the material to be shaped by their art." He further explains that "this means over the formlesss matter, signified by water, just as the love of artists moves over the materials of their art, in order that out of them artists might form their work." He exegetes the biblical phrase "God saw that it was good" to signify that God is pleased with creation, "just as all artists take satisfaction in their art."

Aquinas sees all creation carrying the mark of creativity, because "things were made like God not only in being but also in acting." Furthermore, "the dignity of causality is imparted even to creatures" (255). Yes! To a special degree, the human creature has been blessed with this "dignity of causality." Do we feel such dignity? Or do we take it for granted, wallowing instead in feelings of powerlessness or victimhood?

We humans are especially marked with the power of creativity. In my book *Creativity: Where the Divine and the Human Meet*, I propose that creativity is the very definition employed by anthropologists for our species. We are bipeds who make things. Those two attributes—walking on two legs and creating artifacts—distinguish our species. Our languages too are profoundly creative and diverse.

According to Aquinas, the human intellect is of such magnitude that we can "conceive an infinite number of things in order to make for ourselves an infinite number of instruments." We make an "infinite variety" of weapons, clothing and other necessities of life because we are endowed "with both reason and our hands." Our intellects are vast and open and free—they have "a form that is not determined to one thing alone, as is the case with a stone, but have a capacity for all forms" (259f). It is amazing that he repeats the word *infinite* so readily when he is describing who we are. We are almost infinite in our creative capacities.

Unfortunately, we must be on our guard, for our powers of choice and creativity can also bring evil into the world. We are not pre-programmed to do the good. We must work at that. "The unjust person is worse than injustice and the evil person worse than a brute, because an evil person can do ten thousand times more harm than a beast, because we can use our reason to devise many diverse evils" (261).

Thus our creativity is a double-edged sword. We can do wonderful and awesome things with it—and we can do evil and awful things. The choice is ours to make. That choice is the very meaning of morality.

We ought to
cherish the body
[and] celebrate
the "wonderful communion"
of body and soul.

11. We ought to cherish the body [and] celebrate the "wonderful communion" of body and soul.*

His whole life long, from his early *Commentary on the Sentences* written at about twenty-eight years of age to his midlife work *De Veritate* and to his final work *Summa Theologiae*, Aquinas waged a fierce battle to rebut the dualism of body and soul, spirit and matter. Throughout his life he never altered his position on this critical and highly debated issue. In so doing, he took on the entire ascetic tradition of the fourth-century church fathers and church councils that, as Rosemary Ruether points out, "tended to equate the dualism of soul or mind over body with the dualism of male over female," which results in "a fearful view of sex and a fanatical misogyny toward women."[13] Consider what boldness this took on Aquinas's part—challenging the entire patristic inheritance on so basic a topic as dualism and misogyny! This battle still wages today, of course, because fundamentalism and patriarchy are philosophies that are built on dualism, while a feminist consciousness opts for nondualism. It was on this issue that Aquinas welcomed Aristotle as a liberator from Platonism's antipathy toward matter. I elaborate on Aquinas's battle on behalf of non-dualism or what today

---

* *Sheer Joy*, 149.

we call feminism in *Sheer Joy* as well as his "clay feet" regarding his misunderstanding of women (38-48).

Aquinas fought tirelessly for non-dualism in opposition to the dualism preached by Plato, Augustine, and even St. Bonaventure, a Franciscan colleague in Paris who first supported Aristotle but then reverted back to Platonism. The battle was very contested, and Aquinas lost the battle with the powers that be after his death (see the introduction). It was precisely his non-dualism—expressed as the "consubstantiality of matter and spirit"—that was condemned on March 7, 1277, three years after his death, when the Corporation of Masters of the University of Paris, meeting under the authority of Bishop Étienne Tempier, condemned 219 propositions—of which twenty were aimed at Aquinas's holistic philosophy of the human person.

Ten years later, the archbishop of Canterbury, Robert Kilwardby, censured thirty propositions, most of which concerned Aquinas's position on the consubstantiality of soul and body, spirit, and matter. It took the canonization of Aquinas in 1323 to remove the cloud of suspicion, but in fact Aquinas's holism never took hold in mainline Christianity. Dualism is important for patriarchy and for running empires and keeping down others and for consumer capitalism in our day. Dualism does not empower—it flourishes as a control mechanism.

Aquinas's holism vigorously opposed the traditional position of a dualism of body and soul, a position that originated with St. Augustine but is not found in the Bible. It is not found there because it is in no way Jewish. As Rabbi Heschel explains it: "Asceticism was not the ideal of the biblical man. The source of evil is not in passion, in the throbbing heart, but rather in hardness of heart, in callousness and insensitivity."[14] Biblical scholar Claude Tresmontant points out that nondualism is intrinsic to the Hebrew language itself. "Precisely because it is not dualist, Hebrew, more than any other language, has an understanding, a love of the elements and of the flesh." He points out how dualism attributes "passions and organic functions to the body, and all that is of a psychological order to the soul. In Hebrew, because there is no dualism, passions, organic functions, sensation, are just as easily related to the soul as they are to the organs and, conversely, thought and sentiments are ascribed to the organs and to parts of the body."[15] Aquinas's non-dualist position, being deeply Jewish, was therefore deeply biblical.

Aquinas rejected the prevalent view of there being a "superior reason" of the mind and an "inferior reason" of the senses upon which Augustine and others built their dualism. It is in that context that Augustine said "spirit is whatever is not matter," but Aquinas took the opposite position: spirit is the élan in everything— including matter. "The name 'spirit' expresses a kind of 'élan' or vital impulse, as when we say that 'love moves us' or 'love urges us' to do something" (141–42). It is also his respect for matter that caused Aquinas to prefer Aristotle over Plato. Aristotle gave Aquinas a template of form and matter, act and potency, spirit and energy that allowed him to honor the *dynamic* within all beings—a dynamic, not a dualism.

Aquinas is explicit about why he preferred Aristotle to Plato—it is because Aristotle does not denigrate matter. Significantly, Aquinas wrote commentaries on *twelve* books of Aristotle and not a single commentary on Plato (or Augustine, for that matter, who was heavily tainted by Plato's dualism). Indeed, historian Carol Quigley has said that Augustine became a "lightning rod" for right-wing political movements in the West for centuries.

Aquinas says: "It belongs to the notion of humanity to be composed of soul, flesh, and bones. A particular human being is composed of this soul, of this flesh, and of these bones." Plato taught that "the human being was soul making use of the body," but Aquinas labels this idea "impossible." Why? Because "animals and people are natural and sensitive beings. This could not be the case if bodies and bodily organs were not integral to their essence." He insists that "sensation is not an operation of the soul only. Therefore human beings are not soul only, but something composed of soul and body."

He elaborates: "No part has the perfection of nature when separated from the whole. . . . Hence the soul, although it can exist and can understand separated from the body, nevertheless does not have the perfection of its own nature when it is separated for the body." Furthermore, "by a congruity of relationship that is required between form and matter, spirit fits in with body more than spirit does with spirit since two spirits are two acts, whereas the body is related to the soul as potency is to act." Indeed, "the soul is more like God when united to the body than when separated from it."

Aquinas draws practical conclusions from this position saying "We ought to cherish the body. Our body's substance is not from an evil principle as the Manicheans imagine, but from God. And therefore we ought to cherish the body by the friendship of love, by which we love God." Here we hear Eckhart's words, "the soul loves the body." Matter is not responsible for evil insists Aquinas, our bad choices are and they do "not come to the soul from the body, but to the body from the soul." It is a law of nature that we should care for our body and it is for this reason that "the sensitive appetite and passion are the subject and seat of the virtues."

Aquinas, unlike Augustine and so many theologians before and after him, does not regret our bodies. Rather, he urges us to "celebrate the wonderful communion (*communio mirabilis)* of body and soul. God fashioned the human body in the disposition that is best suited for a rational soul and its activities, for the proximate purpose of the human body is the human soul." And the soul, since it is integral to human nature "has its natural perfection only as united to the body." In no way is sensation "an activity of pure soul—sensation is not unique to the human—we share it with animals. But "it is truly human. A person is not just soul, but a compound of body and soul." And we are made of many elements (today we would say atoms and molecules) that we also share in common with other beings.

Every truth
without exception—
and whoever may utter it—
is from the Holy Spirit.

12. Every truth without exception—and whoever may utter it—is from the Holy Spirit.[*]

These words from Aquinas were written late in life. No doubt he was looking back on his many battles over his eagerness to interact with ideas of non-Christians—including but not limited to Aristotle, Moses Maimonides, Avicenna, Averroes, Plato, and Boethius.

It is difficult to imagine a more ecumenical statement than "Every truth without exception—and whoever may utter it—is from the Holy Spirit." He is saying that truths from *all* the religious traditions of the world are "from the Holy Spirit" and therefore are to be taken in and listened to and meditated on. They can all lead us to the divine, and this is why study is so important a spiritual practice to him (as it is in the Jewish tradition).

Aquinas is also saying that all truth arrived at by science "comes from the Holy Spirit." Thus it is so important not only to pursue science and link it with love of wisdom but also to listen and learn from scientists who help to reveal the insights and revelation that creation contains.

Aquinas also reminds us that all music that speaks

[*] *Sheer Joy*, 31.

truth—all art, all architecture, all mathematics, all novels, all poetry, all dance, all rituals, all films, all documentaries, all political punditry that arrives at truth—is to be taken in and contemplated deeply. Art too, is content worthy of the *lectio divina.*

Aquinas honors the dignity of work. He insists that the politician must know more about the human soul than the physician knows about the body. He honors the vocation of the politician, but he also warns that politicians can bring about great harm. Consider in the last century how successful Adolf Hitler was and how very knowledgeable about the German soul to which he appealed so successfully by appealing to the *resentment* that was harbored there. Aquinas would give him good grades for knowing the soul, but of course flunk him for failing to appeal to what is best in the soul (rather than the evil that is latent there).

Aquinas celebrates work as integral to the Via Creativa, and he insists that the Holy Spirit is always alive and active, inspiring us in all our work and creativity and bringing forth truths from all of our professions and pursuits.

He is speaking of our relationship with other species because they, too, speak truth to us. They, too, are *logos*, the word of God, just as all beings are another Christ, a Cosmic Christ (see chapter 3).

We are surrounded by truth, truth seekers, and truth tellers. Truth reveals itself to us on a daily basis. And it all comes from the Holy Spirit who clearly, in Aquinas's estimation, did not retire after Pentecost but still unleashes revelations today.

Aquinas is in love with truth and truth-seeking. He is a hunter-gatherer after truth, a model and saint and doctor of the church who fulfills that very important archetype of the hunter-gatherer that I wrote about in my book *The Hidden Spiritualty of Men: Ten Metaphors to Awaken the Sacred Masculine.* Aquinas is a walking archetype and story of our pursuit for truth. All his life he sought truth, whether by way of science or philosophy, observation or contemplation, the scriptures or the theologians commenting upon them.

The motto of the Dominican Order to which Aquinas belonged for thirty years is *Veritas.* Truth. We remember some Dominicans for their honest commitment to that pursuit: Thomas Aquinas and Meister Eckhart, Catherine of Sienna and Fra Angelico, Giordano Bruno, Bartholomé de las Casas. And in the twentieth century there is Fr. Marie-Joseph Lagrange, founder of the École Biblique, the oldest biblical and archaeological school in the Holy Land, as well as the scholars there, including Roland de Vaux and Pierre Benoit. And there are theologians who played prominent roles in the Second Vatican Council, such as M.-D. Chenu and his students Yves Congar and Edward Schillebeeckx.

Of course there have also been shadow-filled Dominicans in history, such as Torquemada, chief inquisitor of the Spanish Inquisition; the coauthors of the manual for torturing and burning witches, the *Malleus Malleficarum*; Johann Tetzel, whose mania for selling indulgences in Germany lit the fire to Martin Luther's revolution; and countless other inquisitors more bent on persecuting truth-seekers than honoring and seeking the truth themselves. The history is mixed. The mission, however, is quite clear: *veritas*. Living up to it has proven to be a challenge. Where courage is in short supply, clearly there is rarely a pursuit of truth, but rather a shouldering up with pleasing powers that be. Truth requires courage. Pusillanimity and the failure to speak truth to power honors neither truth nor the Holy Spirit.

In the sentence that heads this chapter, Aquinas gives a green light to every scientist, artist, prophet, and activist to carry on the work of the Spirit, which is always a work of truth. He walked his talk—and he paid a price for it, not only by the controversies he stoked in his lifetime but by way of the condemnations that arose immediately upon his death.

Here we may also mention the "year of silence" he

underwent during the last year of his life, when he put down his pen and was rendered mute right up to the end. Call it a nervous breakdown, call it a stroke, call it a mystical experience—or call it all three—the lesson he leaves behind is clear. "Everything I have written is straw," he exclaimed. These words are an ultimate act of letting go, signified by his inability to finish his *Summa Theologiae.* Compared to the truth he studied, even his genius seemed to offer nothing but straw.

Revelation
has been made to many pagans. . . .
The old pagan virtues
were from God.

13. Revelation has been made to many pagans. . . . The old pagan virtues were from God.*

It is clear from the sentence above that Aquinas is a deep ecumenist, a man of interfaith commitment open to learning how the Spirit works through all religions and cultures.

I am particularly moved by this observation from Aquinas because I have been so richly blessed in my life by so-called "pagan traditions." For example, the Native American tradition—the Lakota tradition, in particular—has grounded and strengthened me and helped keep me on my spiritual path. I have never considered this gift to be anything but supportive of deepening my own Christian roots. I am speaking of sweat lodges that purify and heal the soul, mind, and body and challenge us to dance to the edge of death and return with a deeper gratefulness toward life. I am speaking of a vision quest that I was invited to undergo by Buck Ghosthorse, my friend and mentor, and how in that vision quest I was visited all night long by many spirits who, he explained, once lived on the land where I was praying and who, he declared, "would support me even if many two-legged ones would not."

I am speaking of my first sun dance, when I was

---

* *Sheer Joy*, 31.

invited to dance within the sacred circle and underwent a world-shattering event when the white sun in the sky beamed like a host at a Mass and the sacred tree—to which sun dancers attached themselves in generous but painful giving—appeared as the cross. The moment grafted my Christian roots with my Lakota roots—they came together with a crash like cymbals rendering a loud sound. Visits from deceased relatives and friends were not unusual in the sweat lodge. (I have spoken at greater length about these and other experiences including my vision quest in my autobiography, *Confessions: The Making of a Post-Denominational Priest*).

I am speaking of lessons taught me by Buck Ghosthorse such as this one: "In our tradition fear is the door in the heart that lets evil spirits in. Therefore all real prayer is about strengthening your heart so that fear remains outside the heart, knocking at the door but not coming in." Or this lesson: "Do you want to know how sacred water is? Go without it for three days."

I am speaking of lessons taught me by Sister José Hobday, a Franciscan sister and a Seneca woman who was raised by her tribe as a storyteller, who taught in my programs for many years and was beloved by students. She introduced me to the Four Directions. She introduced me to many rituals that opened the heart, including circle dancing to the drum, the heartbeat of the universe. And the marvelous ritual of pelting with flowers, which we enacted on a number of special occasions. One of these was the celebration of the twenty-fifth anniversary of M. C. Richard's classic work on art as meditation, *Centering: In Pottery, Poetry, and the Person.* M. C. was so deeply moved by the ritual that she wrote a poem, "Pelted by Beauty," describing the event as a "magical ecstasy moving, as the poem sings, through the body into a new behavior."[16]

Sister José taught me deep lessons by her very life and response to life. She had nine brothers, was the youngest child (and the only girl), and was raised on an Indian reservation in Colorado. Eight of her brothers were killed in wars—World War II, the Korean War, and Vietnam. One brother remained, and he was a brilliant engineer who was hired by the government to work on the stealth bomber. One day Sister José received a call from a general who said, "Your brother is dead. Do not pursue any inquiries." It turned out that many persons who had worked on the stealth bomber suffered mysterious deaths after the task was finished— no doubt to keep it all secret. She was very scared and got into her car and disappeared for two weeks. Notice the lesson: Her family gave all its sons to America. Have the native people received anything comparable in return and in gratitude?

One day as a young teenager, José was in a foul mood and acting grumpy all around the house. Her father said: "Get an apple and a blanket and follow me." She disgruntledly obliged and got in the car where he drove her to a cliff in a particularly desert-like part of the reservation. "Get out," he said. "And take your blanket and apple with you. Until you can learn to live with yourself, you are not fit to live with anyone else," and he drove away. She exited the car, blanket and apple in hand, and was so angry that she threw the blanket down the cliff. And the apple followed. After a few hours she got hungry. She climbed down the cliff to retrieve her apple. Then she got cold and climbed down the cliff again to retrieve her blanket.

A wise story about solitude, wouldn't you say?

Yes, so-called "pagan" teachings are not without deep truths that lead to transformed hearts, as well as to actions, stories, and practices that can transform others.

Another so-called "pagan" teacher in my life has been Starhawk, who identifies with the Wicca tradition. She was on my faculty for a number of years and taught courses on ritual-making, which always had a strong component of play and celebration—elements often lacking in Christian worship of late. She also wrote some fine books, such as *Dreaming the Dark*, which treats the Via Negativa in considerable depth, and *The*

Spiral Dance. Starhawk was raised in an orthodox Jewish tradition, but as a teenager she discovered the women's movement and all it might mean to girls and women (and men, for that matter). It took great courage to enter the study and practice of Wicca, but she has touched many people's lives for years—mine included. Her spiral dance at the solstice draws hundreds of people to a lengthy ritual of celebration and seriousness in the passing of the seasons.

She also has worked prophetically in both the permaculture movement and in Palestinian-Israeli peacemaking. Though a Jew herself, she lived for many months with a Palestinian family in Gaza while active in the peace movement. Her close friend, Rachel Corrie, with whom she had trained in non-violent action was murdered by being attacked by a bulldozer driven by an Israeli soldier while engaging in nonviolent peace work in Israel. In short, she is a prophet who has walked her talk and continues to do so.

One of the objections from the Vatican about my work was that she was on my faculty in my creation spirituality program. Whenever Cardinal Ratzinger wrote to my provincial about me, he would add "And he has a witch on his faculty." I once told Starhawk that she was clearly keeping the Vatican up at night. To which she replied: "I don't know why they are threatened by us. We didn't burn any of them at the stake."

I also want to acknowledge the wisdom and knowledge received from the teaching of Yoruba priestess Luisah Teish over the years, who taught African dance and ritual, and who especially opened my heart and mind to the depths of the meaning of "ancestors" and of the goddesses of Africa. Her book *Jambalaya*, as well as her other writings, hold some of the rich teachings of her African tradition.[17]

All this and much more Aquinas is telling us when he says: "Revelation has been made to many pagans. . . . The old pagan virtues were from God." Many "pagan" teachers have taught me virtues by the example of their lives, as well as wisdom from their teachings and rituals.[18]

Every being
is a name for God;
And no being
is a name for God.

14. Every being is a name for God; and no being is a name for God.[*]

This amazing observation Aquinas penned as a very young theologian—it is found in his first book, a commentary on Denys the Areopagite's book *On the Divine Names of God.* Denys lists forty-two names for God taken from the Scriptures including: God as good, beautiful, wise, beloved, eternal, manifest, bestower of life, wisdom, reason, virtue, powerful, salvation, justice, constellation, star, fire, water, air, dew, cloud, stone, rock, etc.

Then Aquinas utters the following: "and all the other beings attributed to God as cause. And the Divine One is none of these beings insofar as God surpasses all things."

One can take such a list of names and add one's own, and in chanting them like a litany or a mantra one takes part in a rich spiritual practice. The Muslim tradition boasts such a practice called "the ninety-nine most beautiful names of God." Inspired by this astounding teaching from Aquinas, I published a book called *Naming the Unnameable*: *89 Most Wonderful and Useful Names for God.* (So as not to compete with the Muslim tradition of 99 names of God, I offer only 89.)

By opening up our minds and hearts to multiple names for God, Aquinas encourages us to let go of stale

---

[*] *Sheer Joy*, 182–83.

and tired God-naming to become young and fresh again in our relationship to the divine. He also encourages our creativity and that of one's culture (including science) to be creative. Or, as one scientist told me, hearing the multiple names for God in my book "takes the top of my head off." In that book I offer names borrowed from the sciences: "Flow, Energy, Spirit, Breath, Mind of the Universe; the Self of the Universe; planetary Mind."[19]

If every being is a name for God because every being can be "attributed to God as cause," then we are not at a loss for alternative and ever more dynamic names for the divine. And, of course, this includes feminine names for divinity as well, including Goddess, Kuan Yin, Osun, Black Madonna, Brown Madonna (Guadalupe), Mother, Wisdom, Shekinah, Gaia, and Tara.

Further names would include Love, Goodness, Beauty, Justice, Compassion, Joy, Laughter, the Cause of Wonder, and the One to Whom We Give Our Thanks.

Judging from the sentence heading this chapter, Aquinas would be on board with all this naming. It is indeed striking that he offers us this feast of divine names in his very first book, written at the age of twenty-eight. Why? Because it demonstrates how thoroughly grounded in nature and creation he was at a young age. It also hints at why he fell in love with a scientist—that is, Aristotle—at so young an age.

The ancient Hindu scriptures tell us that God has "a million faces." Aquinas does them one better—he speaks of *trillions of names*, since for him every being can be a name for God.

Elsewhere he says that "God is pure existence. The existence of all other things partake of God's." And again, "'The One Who Is' determines no particular mode of being. Rather it is indeterminate to all. Therefore it denominates the infinite ocean of being" (87). One might say that God is an infinite ocean of being in which we all swim around.

All the names offered above, whether from Denys the Areopagite, Aquinas, or myself, invoke a Cataphatic Deity. This means a God of light, a God who is revealed in creation, which is made of light, and whom we encounter in a special way in the light of day when we see the beauties of nature all around us.

But there is another dimension our God talk, one that is often neglected: the Apophatic Deity, the God of darkness, mystery, and unknowability. Aquinas refers to this God when he proclaims that "the Divine One is none of these beings insofar as God surpasses all things." I offer nine such apophatic names in my book. As evident in the next chapter, Aquinas offers an understanding of the apophatic divinity that is profound.

We are united
to God
as to
One Unknown.

15. We are United to God as to One Unknown.*

Aquinas has much to say about the Apophatic Divinity. "The cause at which we wonder is hidden from us," he writes. We can and do wonder, and wonder is the beginning of our spiritual journey. But the cause of what we wonder at is hidden behind a veil of mystery.

We also "are united to God as to one Unknown." God is, therefore, "the Unknown One." Aquinas insists upon the transcendence of the divine, but he does not define the divine transcendence in a lazy fashion. For him God is not transcendent because divinity is "out there" some place or far away or up in the sky. No! For Aquinas, "God is closer to us than we are to ourselves." And "God is in all things in the most intimate way" (87).

God is transcendent, says Aquinas, because God is "far beyond anything we think." God is so profound that we cannot go there. "God alone knows the depths and riches of the Godhead, and divine wisdom alone can declare its secrets." There are secrets that only the divine knows. Sometimes we can partake of those secrets, but rarely and by invitation only. We call it grace. We call it revelation. Eckhart called it "breakthrough," in which we learn "that God and I are one."

---

* *Sheer Joy*, 195.

Says Aquinas: "There is something about God that is altogether unknown to persons in this life, namely what God is. For this reason Paul found in Athens the altar inscribed to an 'unknown God.' This is so because human knowledge begins from those things that are connatural to it, that is from creatures known from sense. Yet these are not proportionate to represent the divine essence."

Humans simply cannot "wrap their mind around God," as Estelle Frankel, psychotherapist and student of Kabbalah (a form of Jewish mysticism), puts it in her important book, *The Wisdom of Not Knowing.*[20] Wisdom is bigger than knowledge. It is often beyond words.

Aquinas lived the Via Negativa, becoming mute for a year up to his death. This was a radical act of letting go, one probably brought on by a stroke. Aquinas discovered the Via Negativa in a special way during the final year of his life when he was struck dumb and tasted silence. Silence reigned. This prolific writer and communicator of knowledge put down his pen forever.

The greatest accomplishment
of the human mind
is to know
that it does not know
who God is.

16. The greatest accomplishment of the human mind is to know that it does not know who God is.*

Aquinas was a great mind, he enjoyed an exceptional exposure to the best thinkers in Western history, and he was voracious in his pursuit of knowledge and truth. For example, he was alive when the Cathedral of Notre Dame was being constructed, and though he obviously admired the talent, intelligence, daring, and engineering skill involved in the architecture and building process (which he often uses as an example of humanity's brilliance), the story is told that he stood in front of the unfinished masterpiece and said: "I would trade it all for one copy of St. John Chrysostom's sermons." A fine example of the hungry intellectual pursuit that drove his soul. His thirst for knowledge was insatiable.

Yet this great seeker after truth and knowledge insists that the human mind's "greatest achievement [is] to realize that God is far beyond anything we think. This is the ultimate in human knowledge: to know that we do not know God."

Clearly, though a profound intellectual, Aquinas was not a rationalist. He was an antirationalist, a mystic who knew that not all knowledge is factual knowledge. Some truths are bigger than human concepts and beyond

* *Sheer Joy*, 196.

human words or reasoning. They come primarily from experience, not from reasoning. "When the psalmist says, 'Taste and see the Lord is good,' he first urges one to experience and he then posits the effect of experience."

What is this experience? "Experience of divine goodness is called taste." Thus we are first to *taste* the divine goodness—the Via Positiva, indeed! Taste comes first. He continues: "In corporeal things there is sight first and then taste; but in spiritual things there is taste first but afterward there is sight, since no one knows who does not taste" (86). In fact, the word *wisdom* both in Latin (the language in which Aquinas wrote) and in Hebrew comes from the word *to taste.* Aquinas is hungry for knowledge, but even more hungry for wisdom. And "no one knows who does not taste."

Aquinas recognizes the vastness of human intelligence when he says that the human mind can "know all things." But he also acknowledges the limits of human reason and intellect when he insists that the *ultimate of our knowing is to know what we don't know—and especially that we do not know who God is.* Aquinas is confronting human arrogance here. In typical Aquinas fashion, he gives us the reason for his observation: "By its immensity the divine essence transcends every form attained by the human intellect."

Silence matters. "God is worshiped in silence. God is beyond all speech." But Aquinas also points out that there are several kinds of silence, not all of them of equal value. "There are various kinds of silences: that of dullness; that of security; that of patience; and that of a quiet heart." Clearly, the "quiet heart" takes precedence.

The first requirement, then,
for the contemplation of wisdom
is that we should take complete possession of our minds
before anything else does.

17. The first requirement, then, for the contemplation of wisdom is that we should take complete possession of our minds before anything else does.[*]

Quieting the heart is the work of meditation. One way we taste wisdom is by way of meditation and contemplation. We have seen how Aquinas and the Dominicans were, like the Franciscans, a radical movement of mendicant friars that consciously and deliberately broke with the centuries-old monastic tradition. The key word for these new movements was "poverty"—it was time, they maintained, to turn one's back on the privileges of monasticism and connect to the poor, as Jesus had.

But what to take from the monastic tradition? What to save from the burning building? Contemplation was part of the training within monasticism that Aquinas underwent from the age of five to sixteen. He cherished it, but he also saw it as only part of a bigger vision for deepening one's spirituality. It was important to put contemplation into action, not to hoard it for oneself.

What is contemplation? Says Aquinas: "Contemplation regards the simple act of gazing on truth." Study and meditation can lead to contemplation for "one reaches the knowledge of truth by applying oneself by one's personal study, and this requires

[*] *Sheer Joy*, 110.

meditation" (80). Studying creatures can open the heart to wonder. "From God's creatures we all are led to wonder at the divine power and in this way to hold God in reverence. The maker is nobler than the things that are made. From wonder comes awe and reverence. In addition, creatures have the capacity to warm our hearts to love the goodness of God." What a rich explanation of the Via Positiva and wonder and awe and reverence lies here! Aquinas cites the psalmist who says "I meditate on all your works, I muse on the work of your hands" (Ps. 143:5), and then comments: "Meditation is indispensable for well-instructed faith."

Contemplation often takes us into the darkness, into a "night that holds the quiet of contemplation, in which there is first the desire of the excitement of love: 'My soul has desired you in your decrees: in the middle of the night I rose up to praise you' (Ps 119). And it signifies the silence of divine consolation" (218).

Aquinas also offers advice about contemplative practice in three steps: (1) "The first requirement, then, for the contemplation of wisdom is that we should take complete possession of our minds before anything else does, so that we can fill the whole house [one's mind or soul] with the contemplation of wisdom." (2) "It is also necessary that we be fully present there, concentrating in such a way that our aim is not diverted to other matters." Focus is everything. (3) "Thus Scripture says: 'Return home quickly and gather yourself together there and play there and pursue your thoughts' (Eccl 32:15-16). To 'gather yourself together there' is to draw together your whole intention" (210). This threefold practice sounds quite Buddhist with its emphasis on silence, presence, and letting be. Playing with wisdom is the key and the goal of an empty mind.

Aquinas teaches that "contemplation concerns ends that serve no ulterior purpose." Aquinas compares contemplation to play when he says: "Play, too, is concerned with ends when you play for the fun of it, though with means to ends when you take exercise in order to keep fit." Contemplation becomes a holiday: "The contemplative life is a kind of holiday. 'Be still and see that I am the Lord' (Ps. 46:10). It is a life lived with divine things." Again, this resonates with Buddhist invitations to mindfulness. Furthermore, it is echoed in Meister Eckhart, who urges people to "love without a why" and "work without a why." One plays without a why.

Contemplation includes being alone and in solitude. "In the contemplation of wisdom we work all the more effectively the more we dwell alone with our selves." Thus the words "return home quickly"—that is, "be eager to return from external things to your own mind, before anything else gets hold of it and any other anxiety distracts it. That is why it says in Wisdom 8:16: 'I will enter my house and find rest with her,' with wisdom, that is." What comes next? "When our interior house is entirely emptied like this and we are fully present there in our intention the text tells us what to do next: 'and play there'" (210).

Aquinas celebrates the "delight" that contemplation brings with it, and he offers a broad understanding of contemplation when he identifies it with the pursuit of knowledge and truth. "Contemplation of the truth befits one according to one's nature as a rational animal: the result being that all people naturally desire to know, so that consequently they delight in the knowledge of truth." But the real goal in contemplation is not just knowledge but wisdom! And the habit (or virtue) of blending both, of one leading to the other. "And more delightful still does this become to those who have the habit of wisdom and knowledge, the result of which is that they contemplate without difficulty." Contemplation is natural and organic when it derives from knowledge and truth-seeking.

Contemplation includes the heart; it is about being in the presence of love and this too brings great delight. "Contemplation may be delightful in respect to its object, insofar as one contemplates that which one loves. Even as bodily vision gives pleasure, not only because to see is pleasurable in itself, but because one sees a person whom one loves. Since then, the contemplative life consists chiefly in the contemplation of God, of which charity is the motive, it follows that there is delight in the contemplative life, not only by reason of the contemplation itself, but also by reason of divine love.

How great is this delight? "This delight surpasses all human delight. . . . Hence it is written (Ps. 34:8): 'O taste and see that the Lord is good.'" There is a kind of circle in contemplation that begins in the appetite and travels to the mind and then back to the heart. "The very delight in the object seen arouses a yet greater love. . . . This is the ultimate perfection of the contemplative life, namely, that the divine truth be not only seen but also loved" (439).

It is a great thing
to do miracles,
but it is a greater thing
to live virtuously.

18. It is a great thing to do miracles, but it is a greater thing to live virtuously.[*]

According to Aquinas, living virtuously is more marvelous than miracles! One might even say such living *is itself a miracle.* It is indeed a marvel (which is the primary meaning of "miracle"), a challenge, and an adventure. Virtuous living is worth a lifetime of effort.

One thing I appreciate about Thomas Aquinas's teachings on ethics and morality is that he does not cheapen human adulthood or belittle our capacity for mature thinking by proposing that morality is about obeying rules all the time. Albert Einstein says a person "must consider it an insult when he is told that his conduct should be motivated by fear of punishment or hope of reward."[21] Aquinas does not overindulge in commentaries on the commandments, nor in threats and fear as a motivation for healthy actions. Instead, he develops a lengthy discussion on the Beatitudes, which Aquinas says "contain the whole process of forming the life of a Christian." There "the whole perfection of our life is contained" (502).[22]

Aquinas celebrates a virtue of *epikeia* which is "knowing when to suspend the rules." He treats adults like adults, and instead of proposing a "rule book" to

---

[*] *Sheer Joy,* 326.

follow he draws on the teachings of a "pagan" in his commentaries on Aristotle's *Ethics* and *Politics*. This is significant for our times, for once again it demonstrates Aquinas's Deep Ecumenism—that as human beings we all struggle with living lives of integrity, and that we can learn from one another. No single tradition or lineage holds all the answers to life's ethical dilemmas. We can and must listen to one another, and sometimes even reach back into our histories to discover wisdom.

Following Aristotle, Aquinas chooses to build his ethics not on shoulds and don'ts, but on *virtues*, which he defines as powers. "Human virtue is a participation in Divine power," he declares (350). He celebrates, therefore, our capacity for prudence and wisdom, for justice and love, for courage and fortitude, and—what strikes me as his favorite virtue—magnanimity.

By inviting us to develop our inner selves along the lines of certain virtues, Aquinas demonstrates that virtue is a lifelong effort. One is never fully there, and circumstances of culture and personal development (including one's wounds and experience) will always affect our decision-making.

The proper objects of the heart
are truth
and justice.

19. The proper objects of the heart are truth and justice.*

Cultural critic bell hooks tells us that "the heart of justice is truth telling."[23] One cannot build justice on falsehoods. Those who are engaged in lies cannot also be engaged in justice-making. Currently our culture seems to be going through a truth crisis with "fake news" and incendiary news and very often cold indifference to the truth. There must be a reason why Satan is called "the father of lies."

To say that the proper objects of the *heart* are truth and justice, as Aquinas does, may strike one as surprising since he is so known for critical and systematic *thought*. Is it not amazing that someone of his intellectual depth would insist upon truth and justice residing *primarily in the heart?*

In fact, this underscores how biblical a thinker Aquinas is, for in Jewish thought the intellect is in the heart, not the head. It is a distinctly modern consciousness that has abandoned such understanding and instead rationalized cognition. Descartes's definition of truth as "clear and distinct ideas" is a good example of this modern philosophical tendency. Despite modern science's unparalleled discoveries and contributions

* *Sheer Joy*, 289.

to our knowledge of the world, its tendency to reduce things to merely quantitative dimensions sucks out many dimensions of reality that feed us and open the door to meaning and to value-making. Science coming on with quantity as so basic an approach to knowledge and fact-finding is part of the modernist trend that is visible in Descartes—and, unfortunately, in our schools and universities.

Einstein himself criticized such thinking when he said that we have been given two gifts—rationality and intuition—and that values lie in the intuition and not in our rational intellect. He cautions us to be wary of too much rationality, for our values do not come from the intellect, but from "intuition and deep feeling, which are the same thing." The intellect provides methods, but it does not construct values.[24]

Of course if we live in a myth (as the modern era did) of a "value-free" approach to truth, then the idea that the truth is in the brain alone buttresses such an empty concept of "value." Science and the HeartMath movement are learning today that the brain is not restricted to the head, but actually operates within the heart itself. For instance, the heart sends more signals to the brain than the brain sends to the heart. The heart, therefore, directly influences emotional processing and higher cognitive faculties such as attention, perception, memory, and problem-solving.[25]

Aquinas seems to have anticipated this modern debate. Of course, much of our scientific method was developed to combat the excessive right-brain approach of allegories and symbols and the resultant sentimentalizing *ad nauseam* invoked by an essentially anti-intellectual medieval culture. This is one reason why Aquinas was so excited to discover Aristotle. Right-brain excess, we might say, is as dangerous as that of the left.

Aquinas sought a middle way where both the rational and the intuitive would find a working balance. Many postmodern thinkers advocate doing the same. But first there must be a break from the idolatry of rationality, an idolatry that has taken over so much education and decision-making in our time. It seems to be part and parcel of patriarchy. Wisdom, which Aquinas celebrated his whole life, is feminine in both the Bible and around the world. Patriarchy banishes wisdom in a quest for naked knowledge. We are now bearing the burden of that one-sidedness as we face an ecological crisis that threatens to destroy the earth as we know it.

A great irony in this whole discussion is how often those "Thomists" who claim to follow Aquinas get completely bogged down in trivial texts and rational debates about unending rational dogmas and declarations that rarely get to the heart at all (where spirituality and passion reside). Those students of Aquinas who know what they are talking about—such as my mentor Père Chenu—remind us that for Aquinas *all morality resides not in the will but in the passions!*[26] This was a very controversial position by Aquinas in the Middle Ages, and it is still controversial today, but it parallels Rabbi Heschel's teaching on the centrality of passions to prophets and explains the emphasis Aquinas puts, as we saw above, on *compassion, which is after all a kind of passion*, along with his teaching on anger (see chapter 24).

That truth and justice reside in the heart therefore is biblical, as Aquinas knew well. It also represents a revolution in our awareness and prefigures a revolution in our educational systems from childhood through professional school. A prophetic upheaval of education is long overdue, and Aquinas could lead the way. In some ways, it is already underway in programs such as the aforementioned HeartMath, which, among other things, has confirmed the hypothesis that the brain is present in the heart itself.

I have offered practices in this educational revolution for over forty years by creating training programs in spirituality that have proven very fruitful.

"Art as meditation" and "body prayer" are integral to that training. Art comes from the heart, after all. And the right part of the brain operates much of the heart, located as it is on the left side of the body. Also, as psychologists Claudio Naranjo and Robert Ornstein proposed in the 1970s, "extrovert meditation" (what I call "art as meditation") is "the way of the prophets."[27] I have written about this extensively in my books *Original Blessing*; *Creativity*; *The A.W.E. Project*; and at dailymeditationswithmatthewfox.org. Above all, I have witnessed over forty years of results by implementing it in my pedagogy for training mystics and prophets. A prophet is a seeker of both truth—Thomas Merton says a prophet cuts through 5,000 knots of lies—and injustice. As Rabbi Heschel tells us, every prophet *interferes*. With what? With lies and injustice.

Rationalism has so dominated the modern era that it took over much of twentieth-century artistic philosophy. In her groundbreaking book, *The Re-Enchantment of Art,* Suzi Gablik speaks about her journey from abandoning the modernist culture of art that she was fed on to another vision of art, one that is about personal and social transformation.

Modern aesthetics, she learned soon enough, was "a small but doctrinaire religion." What are its dogmas? "I was trained to view art as a specialized pursuit, devoid of practical or social goals. The concept of 'art for art's sake' was primary. . . . [Its] patriarchal philosophy declared art to be self-sufficient and 'value-free.'"

Spanish philosopher José Ortega y Gasset, a kind of guru of the modernist movement, declared that modern art was "a thing of no consequence" with no social function to perform. Gablik fought against this philosophy and its "core truths of secularism, individualism, bureaucracy and pluralism—all of which in our society *have reduced the mythic and the sacred to rags.*" Art succumbs to the values of the society at large which pursues "manic production and consumption, and the maximizing of profits." Sadly, these become the "ultimate goals for the artist too." A "certain moral lapse occurs." What claims to be "value free" is instead value uncritical and thus succumbs uncritically to the dominant values of a culture.

Gablik abandoned this materialistic philosophy in favor of other values—a "sense of community, an ecological perspective, and a deeper understanding of the mystical and archetypal underpinnings of spiritual life." Art can actually be, she discovered, a "creative work in service to the whole, a philosophical framework for artists who see themselves as agents of social change." She declares that "the great collective project has, in fact presented itself. It is that of saving the earth." Time to make art "as if the world mattered" she says. Interconnectedness becomes an underlying new value. Therefore compassion becomes an underlying new value.

She developed groups for "deep listening" and recognized her new philosophy as a more "feminine" way of operating.[28] Art can be service-oriented instead of self-oriented, as she came to learn.

Is Suzi Gablik's journey in the late twentieth century an echo of Aquinas's teaching in the thirteenth—that "the proper objects of the heart are truth and justice?" Is this one more instance of a premodern consciousness instructing the postmodern?

If truth and justice are the proper objects of the heart, then there is no room for sentimentalism, which is, as Anne Douglas has demonstrated, what happens when justice gets repressed. It is "rancid political consciousness," as she puts it. It is the opposite of real religion and real spirituality.[29]

**The vision of God
is arrived at
through justice.**

20. The vision of God is arrived at through justice.*

All of us seek a vision of the divine. How does that come our way? Contemplation on the beauties of nature and contemplative practice may be one route, and creativity is another, but for Aquinas another route is the Via Transformativa, the way of working for justice and compassion. "God is Justice," he reminds us, and justice itself can be a doorway to the divine, for "the vision of God is arrived at through justice."

Thomas Aquinas was a champion for justice, and he urges the rest of us to get on board. In his day there was plenty of injustice and corruption to address both within the ecclesial establishment and beyond. A veritable battle was waging between the monastic establishment—so tied up with the feudal system that was losing its power and failing to reach the young— and the new mendicant orders.Aquinas did not flinch from the battle. So, too, he sparked theological fires by daring to bring Aristotle, a "pagan" scientist, into the heart of Christian theology. His teachings on justice lay a powerful groundwork for a philosophy of the environment and eco-theology.[30]

One reason Aquinas gives for calling justice the

---

* *Sheer Joy*, 419.

"greatest" of the moral virtues is that justice concerns our relationship with others—"justice is in a way the good of another person." Justice opens the door to the kingdom and queendom of God; it "leads to the reign of God" for Jesus, in preaching the coming of the reign of God, "did not come to call the just to penitence, but to greater justice." Justice is intrinsic to holiness for "the saints have a heart full of justice. . . . The saints have justice, charity, and effects of this kind, which are most like God--they know more than the others."

Aquinas tells us that the prophet Isaiah is busy talking about two things—"justice, which he possesses, and a vision of God. And they follow one upon another. For the vision of God is arrived at through justice. Consider Psalm 15: 'Who will dwell in your tabernacle. One who walks without blemish and exercises justice.' Moreover, 'The gates of life are the gates of justice.'"

Injustices so often reign, but "God is not the originator of injustice." Rather, the "roots of just desire" begin with "delight in God through love." The Via Positiva, therefore, forms the foundation for a life of justice-making. Aquinas cites Paul's letter to the Philippians: "Always take joy in God" (Phil 4:4).

He urges justice-makers, those fighting for justice, "to take pleasure in doing just deeds," and this should flow readily for those who love justice. Why? Because "everyone finds pleasure in what they are fond of. As lovers desire the object that is absent, so they take pleasure in it when it is present. In this way a lover of horses finds pleasure in a horse, and a lover of shows in a show." In fact, virtue is easier when one enjoys doing it. "To the extent that the just love justice, they will take pleasure in doing just deeds. . . . No one will call that person just who does not rejoice in doing just deeds." We see here how profoundly the Via Positiva and Via Transformativa are joined in Aquinas's understanding. The justice-maker is not only in love with the earth but learns to love fighting on behalf of the earth.

"The vision of God is arrived at through justice" means that the Via Transformativa and the work of justice are a means to the vision of the divine. After all, "God is justice" and "God is compassion" for Aquinas. The struggle for justice is a revelation of the divine. Each of the four paths—the Via Positiva, Via Negativa, Via Creativa, and Via Transformativa—bring us to the vision and experience of the divine.

Compassion is the fire
that Jesus came
to set on the earth.

21. Compassion is the fire that Jesus came to set on the earth.*

While Aquinas is happy to talk about contemplation and to practice it, for him contemplation is not the culmination of the spiritual journey. Rather, compassion is the goal. Indeed, this one topic was the single most important conflict between the monastic tradition that had dominated for eight centuries and the new upstart "mendicant orders" of Francis and Dominic. Aquinas talks about the conflict: Share the light, he says! "It is a greater thing to give light than simply to have light, and in the same way it is a greater thing to pass on to others what you have contemplated than just to contemplate" (287).

Aquinas celebrates our powers for compassion: "In itself compassion takes precedence over the other virtues, for it belongs to compassion to be bountiful to others, and, what is more, to succor others in their wants." Compassion is our imitation of God: "Compassion is accounted as being proper to God" and renders divinity "manifest" (395–96). Compassion bears witness to the divine: "Of all the virtues that relate to our neighbor, compassion is the greatest" and it "likens us to God as regards similarity of works. For "the sum total of the

---

* *Sheer Joy*, 401.

Christian religion consists of compassion as regards external works."

Justice and compassion go together for "the will of Christ is twofold—namely, of compassion and of justice." Thus Christ is about two things—compassion and justice. "Compassion does not destroy justice, but in a sense is its fulfillment." Indeed, he declares that "in a certain way compassion is Christ himself."

Why does Aquinas call compassion "the fire the Lord came to send on the earth" (Luke: 12:49)? "Because compassion proceeds from love of God and neighbor which is a consuming fire." He invokes the prophet Isaiah, who says "his tongue is like fire. . . . charity is called a fire primarily because it illuminates. . . . secondly, because it warms." He cites Proverbs: "It is more pleasing to God to show compassion and justice than to offer sacrifice" (Prov 21:3) and Hosea: "I desire compassion and not sacrifice" (Hos 6:6). How can one overcome a hard heart? "The Holy Spirit dissolves the hardness of hearts, as Luke 12 puts it: 'I have come to send fire on the earth" (423). Furthermore, he teaches that "the first effect of love is melting." Thus the Holy Spirit melts the heart through the fire of love.

Aquinas teaches that justice, truth, and compassion "are the same in essence," and he offers this image taken from the psalms. "The psalmist compares justice to mountains, truth to clouds, which are higher, and compassion to the skies, which are higher than all things." "God is justice" he says, and "the most just." Furthermore, "justice is the chief of the moral virtues. By it one is directed in one's relations toward another." In doing justice we "imitate God" as "we imitate God by being compassionate because compassion is bound to accompany love. 'Be you compassionate as your Creator in heaven is compassionate' (Luke 6:36). And this must be in deed" (505). Compassion is not just a pious work or an object of meditation—it requires deeds.

"We find these two things, compassion and justice, in all the works of God. . . . Compassion without justice is the mother of weakness. And therefore it is necessary that they be joined together according to Proverbs 3:3: 'Compassion and truth will not forsake you.'" Aquinas defines compassion this way: "To be compassionate is to have a heart that suffers from the misfortune of others because we think of it as our own. . . . You are truly compassionate when you are eager to repel the misfortune of others" (391–92).

**Conscience
is more to be obeyed
than authority
imposed from the outside.**

22. Conscience is more to be obeyed than authority imposed from the outside.[*]

Conscience plays a central role in Aquinas's teaching about morality. We are to develop a conscience and live by it. The passages in Aquinas about conscience always struck me deeply as I grew up in a very Protestant culture in the 1950s, as I heard time and again that it was Martin Luther who "invented" conscience as the bottom line in morality. "Here I stand," Luther said, taking on the dark forces of the sixteenth-century Roman Catholic Church and peddling of indulgences . Movies, theater, and literature have praised Luther for his sense of conscience, and some commentators have spread the impression that he even invented the concept.

Without diluting Luther's invocation of conscience, consider these teachings from Aquinas three hundred years earlier:

> Conscience is more to be obeyed than authority imposed from the outside. By following a right conscience you not only do not incur sin but are also immune from sin, whatever superiors may say to the contrary. To act against one's conscience and to disobey a superior can both be sinful. Of the two, the first is worse since the

[*] *Sheer Joy*, 474.

> dictate of conscience is more binding than the
> decree of external authority.

He elaborates: "Every judgment of conscience, be it
right or wrong, be it about things evil in themselves
or morally indifferent, is obligatory in such a way that
anyone who acts against their conscience always sins."

To go against conscience—even a mistaken one—is
to "contravene the law of God."

What Aquinas teaches here is not an abstraction.
Dr. Martin Luther King Jr. invoked Thomas Aquinas's
teachings about conscience in his celebrated "Letter from
Birmingham Jail," which soon became the blueprint
for the American civil rights movement. In addressing
the question of civil disobedience, King first declares:
"There are two types of laws: just and unjust. I would
be the first to advocate obeying just laws. One has not
only a legal but a moral responsibility to obey just laws.
Conversely, one has a moral responsibility to disobey
unjust laws." He offers a strategy for distinguishing
between the two: "A just law is a man-made code that
squares with the moral law or the law of God. An unjust
law is a code that is out of harmony with the moral law."
It is at this point that King invokes Aquinas: "To put it
in the words of Thomas Aquinas: An unjust law is a
human law that is not rooted in eternal law and natural

law. Any law that uplifts human personality is just. Any law that degrades human personality is unjust."[31] Aquinas teaches that a "tyrannical law is not a law strictly speaking but rather a perversion of law. . . . Such laws do not bind in conscience" (480).

I know that Aquinas's teachings on conscience informed my decisions when I was being ordered by my Dominican provincial and the Master General in Rome to abort my work with creation spirituality in California. Indeed, I wrote a letter to my Master General in which I cited the passages above apropos of conscience from Aquinas. He never responded to me however. Instead he formally dismissed me from the Order and sent me on my way to become an Episcopal priest and which in my autobiography *Confessions* I call a "Post-denominational priest."

The prophet's mind
is moved
not only to apprehend something,
but also to speak
or to do
something.

23. The prophet's mind is moved not only to apprehend something, but also to speak or to do something.[*]

Speaking of justice, compassion and conscience is to speak of the work of the prophet. Aquinas has a deeply developed theology of the prophet. As Rabbi Abraham Heschel teaches, the prophet commits to interfering with injustice. Aquinas talks about how the prophet Jeremiah "first promises deliverance from evil" and then "freedom from servitude." "'And it will be on that day . . . I will break the yoke,' which is Nebuchadnezzar himself. 'And they will not be dominated.'" And Isaiah says, "'For you have broken the yoke of his burden, and the bar upon his shoulders, and the rod of his oppressor'" (454).

In his *Commentary on Jeremiah*, he writes: "A prophet has been consecrated to overturn, root up, destroy, and again to build and renew." He attributes the work of prophecy to the Holy Spirit when he say "The Holy Spirit is the spirit of prophecy, as Joel says (2:28): 'I shall pour out my spirit upon all flesh and your sons and your daughters shall prophesy.'" But the Holy Spirit is omnipresent, and so too is the vocation to be prophets. All are called to do what prophets do, which

---

[*] *Sheer Joy*, 470.

is to stand up to injustice and struggle for healing and justice.

The prophet needs to develop one's strength in order to overcome "fear of the world." This strength comes from love for "fear makes peoples slaves, loves sets them free" notes Aquinas. (453) It is saintly and part of holiness to work for justice and peace. "Take note of the saying in Isaiah, 'the work of justice will be peace. . . .' The saints reckon three things in regard to the peace that they desire. First, the strength of divine power. Psalm 125 says: 'Those who believe in the Lord are like Mount Sion which will never be shaken. . . .' Second, the purity of one's own conscience, as in Proverbs 3: 'You will walk confidently along your way, and your foot will not stumble.' Third, the removal of hostile evil, as in John 16: 'Be confident, I have overcome the world'" (454–55).

Aquinas counsels us to be like the prophets who face fear and become strong, first, by submitting to divine power in sacred experiences of creation (such as mountaintops); second, by following one's conscience and developing trust in that way; and, third, by daring to remove hostile evil, again by way of trust and confidence. It is significant how he invokes trust or confidence twice in this passage. When I asked a prophet within the civil rights movement, Fred Shuttlesworth—a minister whose home was bombed by the Ku Klux Klan and was beaten with chains multiple times—where he got his courage he said to me: "You can call it courage; but I call it *trust.*"

Trust is, of course, the real meaning of faith as invoked by Jesus in the gospels. It is the primary meaning of the word *faith*—which is not about believing in a series of dogmas but about believing in the presence of the Spirit when one stands up for justice and pays the consequences. Shuttlesworth knew this, and Aquinas knew this.

What is the primary work of the prophet? "The prophet's mind is moved not only to apprehend something, but also to speak or to do something; sometimes indeed to all these three together, sometimes to two, sometimes to one only." The prophet sees injustice and stands up to be counted; the prophet speaks out; the prophet does the work necessary to make transformation happen. The prophet, moved by the Holy Spirit, often does not even know what is at stake. "Since the prophet's mind is a defective instrument, even authentic prophets do not know all that the Holy Spirit means by the things they see, or speak or even do."

Aquinas anticipates Rabbi Heschel's classic study, *The Prophets*, as well as Walter Brueggemann's *The Prophetic Imagination*, when he insists that creativity and imagination play a prime role in the work of the prophet. "A way of speech is opened up that proceeds by way of metaphors and figures, which is the proper mode of prophets. Numbers 12 says: 'If someone shall have been a prophet of the Lord among you, I will appear to them in a vision, and through dreams I will speak to them'" (462). The prophet listens to his or her dreams.

Says Aquinas: "It is characteristic of prophets to reveal what is not present but hidden. . . . The act of prophecy is to know hidden things and to announce them." The prophet looks ahead and speaks out before others for "the prophet is said to be not only one who speaks from afar, that is, one who announces, but also one who sees from afar, for the Greek *phanos*, which is an appearing."

Aquinas recognizes two acts in the prophetic vocation: "one is primary, namely, sight; and the other is secondary, namely, announcing. The prophet does the announcing either by words or even by deeds, as is clear in Jeremiah (13:5). . . . But in whichever of the two ways the prophetic announcing is made . . . [it] takes place through certain outward signs." Those signs come from the imagination and from art. Such lively images awaken others. Announce what is hidden or forgotten or lying in denial.

The prophet Jeremiah, Aquinas points out, refused

"to be silent." The prophet speaks out. Compassion is integral to the prophet, "Jeremiah expresses the compassion of the prophet, saying, 'since if you have not heard, your soul will lament in secret." Prophets feel deeply the suffering of the people. "Isaiah 22 says: 'Withdraw from me, I will weep bitterly. Don't come to console me about the destruction of the daughter of my people."

The gift of prophecy is not a private gift and certainly not a gift for one's ego. Rather, "prophecy is given not for the prophet's sake but for the building up of the church." (At one place Aquinas defines the church as "a garden.") On the other hand, this same gift can benefit oneself *and* others at the same time, for "sometimes the gift of prophecy is given to people both for the good of others and in order to enlighten their own mind." The prophetic grace permeates all of society for "the prophetic light extends even to the direction of human acts; and in this way prophecy is requisite for the government of a people, especially in relation to divine worship, since for this nature is not sufficient and grace is necessary" (454).

Saints are prophets, Aquinas declares, for three reasons. First, "they were inspired by God. Joel 2 says: 'I will pour out my spirit over all flesh and your sons and daughters shall prophesy.'" "Second, because they were sent by God, Matthew 23 says: 'Behold, I send to you prophets, and wise peoples, and scribes.' Isaiah 29 says: 'And now the Lord and his spirit, have sent me.'" "Third, since they witnessed to God (Acts 10): 'All the prophets give witness to God.' Isaiah 44 says: 'You are my witnesses.'" There is also a "fervent feeling shown by their communal charity, of which he says: 'Here is one who loves the brotherhood'" (465).

Prophetic revelation does not happen all the time for a prophet; it comes and goes and depends on the disposition of a person to receive it. "'We prophesy in part,' that is, imperfectly." No one prophet has all the answers—"The Lord reveals to the prophets all things that are necessary for the instruction of the faithful; yet not all to every one. But some to one, and some to another." Furthermore, "prophetic light is not something abiding in the prophet, but a kind of transient impression." Prophets are not prophets twenty four hours a day. "Just as the air is ever in need of a fresh enlightening, so too the prophet's mind is always in need of a fresh revelation."

Aquinas honors women who were prophets. He calls Mary, the mother of Jesus, a "prophetess who prophesized saying, 'My soul magnifies the Lord' (Luke 1). God approached her through prophetic intelligence and through faith." Of course he is alluding to the deeply prophetic poem ascribed to Mary known as the Magnificat (Luke 1:46-55), which sings of how God "has routed the proud of heart, pulled princes down from their thrones and exalted the lowly" (Luke 1:51-52).

Aquinas says: "The Holy Spirit is called a prophetess, who is the beginning of all prophecy, 2 Peter 1 says; 'For it is not by human will that prophecy is brought forth, but inspired by the Holy Spirit the saints, men and women of God, have spoken.'" Aquinas reminds us of a point that contemporary feminists have been making—namely, that spirit is feminine. "For among the Hebrews 'spirit' is in the feminine gender, namely 'Ruah' and respecting this, 'Mary conceived,' that is, the Spirit made her to conceive. For that which 'has been born in her is from the Holy Spirit'" (465).

Aquinas also celebrates Mary Magdalene as a prophet. "A triple privilege was placed upon Mary Magdalene. First, prophecy, because she deserved to see the angels, for prophecy is between the angels and the people." And "the apostolic office to be sure. She became the Apostle of the apostles, because the announcement of the Lord's resurrection to the disciples was entrusted to her." Aquinas praises her boldness: "Mary says to the gardener: 'Tell me where you have laid the body of Jesus and I will take him away.' The boldness of the woman is amazing! It removes the fear of the sight of a dead person and impels her to try to do more than she is able, that is, to carry away the corpse. This is what Paul means in 1 Corinthians 13.7: 'Love hopes all things.'"

Courage and boldness are integral to the work of the Holy Spirit that anoints the prophet. This applies to all of us coming to all of us as we come to our maturity as spiritual adults.

In speaking of the prophets Aquinas leaves us with a startling observation when he says: "The doctrine of both apostles and prophets is necessary for salvation" (472). First, he insists that those who interfere with injustice are leaving us "doctrines"—that is, teachings of orthopraxis, or how to live the gospel teachings properly. Second, he tells us that prophets are equal in importance to bishops. We should, therefore, listen to the prophets—and not just the ecclesial poobahs. Might that make for a whole new version of "church"?

A trustworthy person
is angry
at the right people,
for the right reasons,
expresses it in the appropriate manner
and for an appropriate length of time.

24. A trustworthy person is angry at the right people, for the right reasons, expresses it in the appropriate manner and for an appropriate length of time.[*]

To speak of justice, as we have in previous chapters, is to speak of injustice and therefore of moral outrage. Such outrage takes place in our third chakra, where we carry our anger and where we feel "kicked in the gut" when we hear of the taking of children at the border from their parents to be put in cages. Or when we hear lies that do not stop from our politicians and presidents; or when we admit the facts about climate change—and its deniers. Or when we see the insane amount of money spent on weapons worldwide ($56,000 per second!), while children starve and youth go without education. (And note that half of that $56,000 is spent by the United States.)

All prophets are angry. It is what they do with their anger that counts and sets them off from the rest of us. Gandhi, Dr. King, and Nelson Mandela all employed a nonviolent strategy that brought forth genuine results. It has proven effective in throwing off an empire (Gandhi), desegregating the South (King), and making for a relatively peaceful transition after years of rigid

---

[*] *Sheer Joy*, 329.

apartheid (Mandela). Prophets tap into the anger of their people and direct it in ways that are *effective*, so that it does not get lost or dissipated. Venting by itself can create more backlash and even violence and thus give birth to still more outrage and anger. This is also why all prophets are artists—they create *social art*, the creative gathering of anger and imagination to transform social structures of thought and action toward the long arc of justice.

As Rabbi Heschel tells us, the prophet is all about passion. "We are stirred by their (the prophets) passion and enlivened imagination. . . . It is to the imagination and the passions that the prophets speak rather than aiming at the cold approbation of the mind."[32]

We are all called to be prophets—people who interfere—just as we are all called to be mystics—people who love (and are therefore angry when what we cherish is threatened).

Aquinas knew this. Unlike many dualistic spiritual teachers, he does not advise people to repress their anger, or sit on it, or dwell incessantly in bliss, or run from the pain of the world, or go into denial about the evil that provokes anger. Rather, he reminds us to treat our anger with respect and find appropriate outlets for it. And not to let it control us ("for the appropriate length of time" he counsels). Invest it! Yes, we should invest our anger—for it is an energy source *par excellence*—in effective action to bring about change.

While anger, of course, must be regulated because it can take over our reasoning faculties and run away from us, when it "follows the judgement of reason it helps toward the execution of reason's command" (422). Anger provides the energy to get something good done even amid obstacles.

Once we have determined the appropriate causes of our outrage at injustice, Aquinas counsels us that art—including social art—represents the "appropriate manner" in which to utilize or invest our anger. From such anger emerge allies who can join us in our action. The word *community*, after all, comes from the Latin words *cum munio*, meaning "to share a common alice

That is what politics is really about. People seeing what is missing in society and banding together to do something about it. From injustice to justice. From outrage to action. From despair to hope. From disempowerment to empowerment. Anger can offer energy for the struggles that ensue. Aquinas knew this. And Jesus knew this, as is evident in the story of his turning the money-lenders' tables over in the temple. Jesus often expressed his anger directly in debates with hypocritical religious powerbrokers and, more subtly, in his artful storytelling and parables. He did not run from his anger, but found a healthy outlet that refused to psychologize it ("Oh, you are so angry, Jesus") and instead reached down to identify its root causes.

Aquinas praises anger when he says: "Nothing great happens without anger." Anger is an energy source that we must tap into—but in appropriate ways and for the appropriate length of time and directed at the appropriate people, just as Aquinas advises. Anger is one of those passions that Aquinas celebrates as being the very place where virtue is born within us.

Aquinas believes that anger is related to injustice— "that which provokes anger is always something considered in the light of an injustice." We are angry because something we love is being threatened or endangered: "If we are angry with those who harm others . . . it is because those who are injured belong in some way to us; either by some kinship or by friendship, or at least because of the nature we share in common" (184).

**Playfulness, or Fun,
is
a Virtue.**

25. Playfulness, or Fun, is a Virtue.*

According to Aquinas, prophets must undergo practices that refresh one's mind, spirit, and body on a regular basis. Aquinas celebrates the virtue of *eutrapelia*, which he defines as "playfulness" and calls for busy people to make room for it: "Words or deeds wherein nothing further is sought than the soul's delight are called playful or humorous. Hence, it is necessary at times to make use of them, in order to give rest, so to speak, to the soul." He calls for resting the soul just as we must rest the body. "Weariness of the soul must of necessity be remedied by resting the soul; and the soul's rest is pleasure." He tells the story of how an archer was asked if he could shoot a bow and arrow "indefinitely," and the archer replied that if he did so "the bow would break." He then concludes: "In like manner a person's mind would break if its tension were never relaxed."

Aquinas urges us to take care of ourselves and to know our limits. The prophet, especially, must be careful because even if the cause is good one cannot "cheat" on our needs to take care of ourselves. One thinks of Meister Eckhart's teaching that "compassion begins at home with one's own body and soul." It is

---

* *Sheer Joy*, 437.

significant that Aquinas declares that "to be playful is part of the virtue of modesty." Acknowledging our need for play respects our limits, recognizing we are all human and in need of play, as well as work. We seek a balance in our lives.

In his commentary on Matthew's gospel, Aquinas goes on at some length when commenting on the following passage: "What description can I find for this generation? It is like children shouting to each other in the market place: 'We played the pipes for you, and you wouldn't dance; we sing dirges, and you wouldn't mourn. . . .' At that time Jesus exclaimed: 'I bless you Father, Lord of heaven and earth, for hiding these things from the learned and the clever and revealing them to mere children. Yes, Father, for that is what it pleases you to do' (11:25)."

Aquinas—like Jesus—sees children as important teachers of how to have fun when he writes: "Children do not have anxieties, so they are free in regard to the things that they seek for themselves: this is playing." Playing is about recovering the sense of freedom we felt as children. It honors the child within us all. And it honors our sense of community, which is integral to our human nature. "Human beings are naturally social, and on account of this, since one naturally needs another, they find pleasure in living together. Thus the

Philosopher [Aristotle] says in *Politics*: 'Every person who is solitary is either more than human and is a god; or is worse than human and is a beast.. . . . Thus it is said in Matthew's gospel 'for those sitting in the marketplace,' because no one wished to play by oneself, but in the forum or meeting place where many gather is where play takes place."

He compares the play of children with the "delight" that adults take in art such as admiring good sculpture. He invokes music for "nothing alters the soul like a song." Speaking of song he reminds us that "where the word stops, there the song begins. The song is the exultation of the mind bursting forth into voice" (263). He invokes Boethius and Pythagoras, as well as the scriptures: "Wine and music gladden the heart" (Eccl 40:20). Music brings us to joy and also to weeping as in Jeremiah 9:17: "Call the mourners, and let them mourn over us" (436).

It is meaningful that Aquinas develops his teaching on fun or playfulness as a virtue in his *Commentary on Isaiah*. He emphasizes how prophets, too—indeed, especially—must play not only so they don't take themselves too seriously amid their significant work, but also so they don't take their work too seriously—though it is serious. This is all part of living and working—as Eckhart teaches—"without a why."

But there is another reason for fun among prophets—namely, that the prophet must develop one's creativity and imagination—and play is integral to such creativity. Here is how Carl Jung put it: "Without this playing with fantasy, no creative work has ever yet come to birth. The debt we owe to the play of the imagination is incalculable."[33]

If play and fantasy are essential for creativity, keeping creativity alive is keeping playfulness alive. Aquinas says: "Since it is impossible to be always engaged in the active and contemplative life, it is sometimes necessary to intersperse joys with cares, lest the mind be broken by too much severity." Furthermore, from this time for fun we return better equipped for work for "in this way a person may be more readily open to virtuous activity."

Aquinas cautions that play and fun come in different modes. Some fun—indulging drug addiction, for instance—is a negative kind of play. But play we must, and if the positive kinds are not part of our daily habits, then we leave ourselves open to the more sinister variety. "It is natural for people to seek after pleasure, and they always seek after it and if it is lost through anxiety, then one immediately rushes into the pleasures of evil."

Not only do we need the virtue of *eutrapelia* for

our own health, but we need it for those around us as well. To interfere with or discourage the play of others Aquinas labels a "sin," because it is against reason. "Now it is against reason for anyone to be burdensome to others by offering no pleasure to them, and by hiding their enjoyment." In fact, Aquinas calls people who lack a sense of humor and cannot laugh "ungrateful boors": "Anyone who is without mirth is not only lacking in playful speech, but is also burdensome to others, since they are deaf to the moderate mirth of others. Consequently they are sinful and are said to be *ungrateful boors.*"

A true prophet is eager to celebrate, love life, laugh at its paradoxes, and turn from seriousness to playfulness. (In fact, as Aquinas notes, the Greek word *eutrapelia* derives from the word *trepein*, meaning to turn.) Celebration is as much a part of compassion as fighting against injustice. Both are necessary to sustain the struggle and to sustain the soul. Celebration is integral to compassion, as Eckhart put it: "What happens to another, whether it be a joy or a sorrow, happens to me."

I am reminded of the time I led a workshop on the Cosmic Christ in an Earth/Spirit conference in Portland, Oregon. Part of my workshop was to invite participants into circle dancing (body prayer, like art as meditation, is excellent for instructing prophets). Afterward, a young man came up to me with this story: "I am a zealot on behalf of the earth," he said. "I chain myself to bulldozers, I lie down in front of them, and I have been to prison more times than I can count. But what we just did—dancing these circle dances—is the most radical thing I have done in my entire life. I can hardly wait to bring them back to my fellow zealots in the woods."

Two years later I ran into him again, and I asked whether he had brought circle dancing to his fellow protestors. "Yes I did," he replied. "And it totally changed our way of protesting. Thanks to the dances we learned to think differently, more broadly, about our task, and we expanded our network to include hunters, for example. We used to consider them our enemies, but through our expanded imaginations from doing dances, we learned they are our allies because they, too, know the game is disappearing." Yes, all politics is about expanding the numbers who stand up and say no. We must anointing additional prophets. If creating requires "fantasy and play," as Jung teaches, then *eutrapelia* is integral to prophetic training.

Another translation for *eutrapelia* might be, more simply, *fun. Eutrapelia* is the virtue of fun. We all need fun in our lives; all prophets need fun in their lives.

Consider Eckhart: "What happens to another whether it be a joy or a sorrow happens to me." Compassion is sharing not only in one another's sorrow, but also in one another's joy and celebration. Compassion is about both justice and love, joy and sorrow, and relieving that sorrow and sharing that joy.

I am struck and inspired by the role that fun plays among young people today—even amid climate change and all the other severe realities that face this new generation. Fun is a value for them. Without fun, our imaginations become stifled, and we cannot escape from the seriousness of the task at hand. Fun is a virtue of our postmodern times, and Aquinas, a premodern citizen, underscores its importance for both the individual and society at large.

Sins of the flesh
take you toward God;
Sins of the spirit
take you away from God.

26. Sins of the flesh take you toward God; sins of the spirit take you away from God.[*]

I was so struck by this statement from Thomas Aquinas that I worked it into the title of my major book on Evil called *Sins of the Spirit, Blessings of the Flesh: Transforming Evil in Soul and Society.* I spend three chapters in the book celebrating what science has told us about flesh and matter and their sacredness, including the wonders of the flesh of the universe, the earth, and our human bodies, all of which we now recognize as made of the same stuff that was given birth 13.8 billion years ago.[34]

What excites me about Aquinas's observation that sins of the flesh take us toward God and sins of the spirit away from God is that this teaching has the potential to end the sexual preoccupations of so much bad religion, a preoccupation that freezes people into a juvenile and adolescent stage of developmental awareness. As Pope Francis observed, there are "anti-condom zealots" who are want to "stick the whole world inside a condom."[35]

Ever since Pope Paul VI's ill-advised encyclical *Humanae Vitae*, there has been drawn a line in the sand regarding whether one is for or against birth control. The Roman Catholic Church has practically split over

[*] *Sheer Joy*, 423.

the issues of sexuality in recent decades, with the right wing making their rallying cry all about birth control—even though 93 percent of Catholics disregard the papal teaching on birth control—or homosexuality.

At the same time—and with no surprise—the loudest among the sexuality enforcers have more often than not succumbed to intense self-hatred, hypocrisy, and arrogance. Prime examples of this reality are laid bare in the recent lengthy study by French journalist Frédéric Martel, *In the Closet of the Vatican*, which concludes that most of the prelates attacking Pope Francis on his efforts to ease up on homophobia are not heterosexual prelates themselves, but self-hating gay prelates hiding in places of power—including the Congregation of the Doctrine of the Faith.

One such figure who appears in Martel's book is Cardinal Burke. A cleric close to Pope Francis states that Burke "is the very thing he denounces starkly." He is "anti-gay and rages against homosexuality" and preaches that you should not "invite gay couples to family gathers when children are present" and homosexual couples are like "the person who murders someone and yet is kind to other people." He denounces the pope for trying to alter the homophobic teachings of the church and calls homosexuality a "grave sin" and "intrinsically disordered." Same-sex marriage is "an act of defiance against God" that derives from Satan. Martel comments that Burke's "homophobia is so intense that it even disturbs the most homophobic Italian cardinals." He "goes literally mad," one Vatican priest observed, "when Pope Francis doesn't wear red shoes or eccentric outfits."[36]

Poet W. H. Auden may have put the issues at stake most succinctly when he wrote: "As a rule it was the pleasure haters who became unjust."

Thomas Aquinas comes down decisively on the side of justice-seeking and of pleasure. He was not a pleasure hater—indeed, he teaches that the practice of virtue increases happiness and pleasure. "Pleasure arising from virtuous activities will be more delightful than any other pleasures. A passion of the soul increases the goodness of an action. . . . The more perfect a virtue is the more does it cause passion" (428). And he absolutely stands for justice as the "primary moral virtue" because it relates us to our neighbor. "The saints have a heart full of justice . . . charity, and effects of this kind, which are most like God" (419). Justice and love go together—but not necessarily love and celibacy. "Perfection does not consist in what is exterior to it, such as poverty, virginity, and the like except when these are instruments of love."

He tells us that "God is justice" and urges us to

"open the gates of justice." There are two kind of gates we encounter in life: the evil ones, "which close the entrance to life," and the good ones, "by which the way of life is opened. Psalm 118 says: 'Open the gates of life,' that is of justice. The evil gates are sins; but the good ones are virtues."

Why does Aquinas insist that sins of the flesh take one toward God? He explains: "Spiritual sins are more grievous than carnal sins other things being equal. . . . Carnal sin as such denotes a *turning toward* something, and for that reason implies a closer cleaving. Whereas spiritual sin denotes more of a *turning from* something, whence the notion of guilt arises. For this reason it involves a greater guilt." A "closer cleaving" might mean more intimacy. Sexual seeking is *a seeking* for intimacy, for cleaving, for love given and received, a yearning for goodness.

Sins of the spirit, on the other hand, are all about *turning away* from something, a flight from our own deepest self and its yearning for the good. Aquinas attributes this turning to "spiritual blindness and hardness of heart [which] imply the movement of the human mind in cleaving to evil and turning away from the divine light." In "spiritual blindness" there lies a closing of the mind and refusal to learn while Aquinas believes learning includes both "sight and discovery." No discovery! No curiosity! A "know-it-all" attitude accompanies sins of the spirit. A stuckness and attachment.

Carnal sins, however, do not turn us away from "the divine light" but toward it in a movement of discovery and curiosity. Desire seeks union, communion, and ecstasy. And therefore a movement toward the divine. Indeed, "prayer is the expression of desire" according to Aquinas (457).

What are some of the "sins of the spirit" that turn us away from the divine light and our deepest and best selves?

Among these sins would be *greed* or *avarice*. Greed separates one from others, expands the ego, and hoards. Aquinas says that a "quest for infinity" resides in all of us, but avarice seeks the infinite in all the wrong places. Avarice often leads to addictions that create havoc in relationships and never truly satisfy the yearning of the soul.

Acedia (often mistranslated as sloth) is a spiritual sadness (despair, depression, boredom, passivity) that robs us of the energy to begin new things or even to care about others.

Hatred is understood as coldness of heart and indifference to others.

Fear, Aquinas teaches, can so take over the human soul that all compassion is driven away.

Violence is anger that is out of control and harms others.

Consumerism would qualify as today's most prevalent version of gluttony. It can gag the throat (*gluttus* means "throat" in Latin).

Arrogance separates us from others such as happens whenever we believe our "tribe" is superior to others. Thus racism, sexism, heterosexism, cold capitalism, excessive nationalism, anthropocentrism (what Pope Francis calls our collective narcissism as a species), adultism—all these are sins of arrogance and, therefore, sins of the spirit—and all of them separate us from one another and from a God of justice and compassion.

I also propose *rationalism* (and the repression of our intuitive or mystical brains) as a sin of the spirit appropriate to the modern era.[37]

Taking on all these shadow forces that allure humans is the work of a strong spirit, a spiritual warrior—which is to say all of us. Part of warriorhood is to be alert. To stay alert about how any or all of these forces can take us over is to stand up to evil both within ourselves and within society and its structures.

Aquinas is a big help in naming the challenge before us. Sins of the spirit that want to cut us off from justice and relationships with others hold far more destructive power to them than sins of the flesh that seek to bring us together ever more intimately.

What if religion had followed Aquinas's teachings instead of the sins of the flesh teachings that mirror the guilt-ridden path of Augustine and company? Clearly it would not be as stuck in childish ways as it is, nor as blind as it sometimes is vis-à-vis social and ecological and structural sins. Psychology has become a healer for many to grow beyond the path of sexual guilt. We can be grateful for that. Psychology is no substitute for justice-making and healthy spirituality, yet it can be a valuable precursor. It can instruct us in needed self-knowledge and recognition of the shadow we all carry. It can assist our efforts to cease projecting and in the process it can empower people to come to their true and deepest selves, to become therefore the lovers and prophets we are all called to be.

It pertains to Magnanimity
to have
a great soul.

27. It pertains to Magnanimity to have a great soul.[*]

Along with the virtues of justice and compassion, Aquinas urges us to magnanimity (from two Latin words, "great" and "soul"). Magnanimity is about acting out of a large soul. In times of stress and chaos—and such chaos will only increase as climate change brings rising oceans, droughts, and massive migrations—we humans must become of stronger and deeper character. In such times magnanimity will be called for, and it is especially important to see it developing in young people. I am bullish about magnanimity, and I especially love to see it in young people.

Aquinas reminds us that "magnanimity is the expansion of the soul to great things. . . . To do something great . . . belongs properly to the very notion of virtue." Of course, the word *magnanimity* comes from the Latin words for "great" and "soul." Thus Aquinas declares that "it pertains to magnanimity to have a great soul" and "magnanimity makes all virtues greater."

Magnanimous people, in Aquinas's understanding, do not depend overly much on the opinions of others. "It is characteristic of magnanimous people to be more solicitous about the truth than about the opinions of

---

[*] *Sheer Joy*, 351.

others. They do not depart from what they ought to do according to virtue because of what people think." Magnanimous people do not hide, for "it is a mark of magnanimous people to speak and work openly . . . and publicly divulge their words and deeds." Furthermore, magnanimity does not hang on to hurts but moves on: "Magnanimous people deliberately determine to forget injuries they have suffered."

People hide what they do or say out of fear, but magnanimity is the opposite of fear—it is an expression of courage. Courage and magnanimity go together: "magnanimity is a part of the virtue of courage or fortitude." In taking on big tasks, magnanimity faces great challenges and obstacles. Hope is very much needed in dark times like ours, so magnanimity is needed also for it "establishes the soul when arduous tasks arise." And because it is "about hope in some arduous task" it is also about *trust.* Trust adds something to hope—it "furnishes a certain vigor to hope. For this reason it is the opposite of fear, as is hope." Vigor, energy, enthusiasm, are part of hope revitalized by trust and magnanimity.

In times of increasing despair like our own, this insight about trust and hope and magnanimity seems especially practical and valuable. A crisis of hope faces us all today. But Aquinas also addresses the cause of despair when he discusses taking on the powers of evil. "Because courage properly speaking strengthens a person against evil, magnanimity strengthens a person to take on good tasks. That is why trust pertains more properly to magnanimity than to courage."

Magnanimity is arduous, it takes effort. "It is difficult for anyone to be magnanimous. No evil person is able to be magnanimous." But the rest of us can be. Apparently evil renders a person smaller in soul, not larger.

While magnanimous people take on large tasks and implement great visions, they do not do so out of naiveté regarding the opposition and the courage that is required to overcome it. Here is how Aquinas puts it:

> Magnanimous people do not expose themselves to dangers for trifles, nor are they lovers of danger, as it were exposing themselves to dangers hastily or lightly. However, magnanimous people brave great dangers for great things because they put themselves in all kinds of danger for great things, for instance, the common welfare, justice, divine worship, and so forth.

It would seem, therefore, that the great movements needed to combat climate change and wake people up to their deeper selves, their prophetic and mystical selves, will demand plenty of magnanimity. To reinvent education, religion, worship, politics, economics, media, engineering, art will require magnanimity. And I know no surer guide than Thomas Aquinas. Indeed, he has been an inspiration in the work I have undertaken with many other people--dj's, vj's, rappers, musicians and more--in creating cosmic masses the past twenty-five years to renew forms of worship. It has demanded magnanimity of us all. It is a great task and has proven rewarding to many. (See http://www.cosmicmass.org)

.

Angels
carry thoughts
from prophet to prophet.

28. Angels carry thoughts from prophet to prophet.[*]

Aquinas has some amazing teachings about angels, or what indigenous people call "spirits." That is one reason British biologist Rupert Sheldrake and I chose Aquinas as one of our principal thinkers with whom to dialogue on the subject (along with Hildegard of Bingen and Denys the Areopagite) in our book *The Physics of Angels*.

One lesson that Rupert found astonishing was that if one substitutes the word *quanta* for "angels," Aquinas's angelology addresses many of the same questions that today's quantum physics asks. "When Aquinas discusses how angels move from place to place, his reasoning has extraordinary parallels to both quantum and relativity theories" (23).

The issues that Aquinas deals with in relation to the movement of angels—continuity, discontinuity, action in place—are similar to the discussion about the movement of photons and other quantum particles in quantum theory. Writes Sheldrake: "Part of my interest in Aquinas's work on angels was awakened precisely by seeing these parallels. I think the parallels arise because he's dealing with the same question: How can something

[*] *The Physics of Angels*, 3. All references in this chapter are to this book.

nonmaterial and indivisible move and act on bodies located in particular places?" (104-105). Yet angels are distinguished from quanta insofar as they employ conscious choice in their movement per Aquinas.

In discussing angels and instantaneous movement, Sheldrake cites Aquinas who says: "The beginning is in one instant and the end in another between these there is no time at all." Sheldrake comments: "Let us say then that [a photon's] movement is in time, but not in the way that bodily movements are" (106). Photons, like angels, can be said to exist in an eternal now where one does not grow old. A photon can be in one place at one instant, as when light leaves the sun and another place at another instant as when the flight from the sun hits something on the earth and lights it up about eight minutes later. *But from the point of view of the photon itself, no time elapses.* And the photon does not age in the process.

Aquinas calls angels "beings of light." Says Sheldrake: "It is not just a coincidence that we find remarkable parallels today between angels and the nature of light." Aquinas reminds us that angels are cosmic beings who assist with the work of the unfolding and evolving universe. Angels are not just about guarding individuals but are instrumental in "governing the universe."

Rupert taught me a story I had never heard before about evolution—namely, that Charles Darwin developed his theory of evolution along with another scientist, Alfred Russel Wallace, and they presented their findings for the first time back-to-back at the Linnean Society of London on July 1, 1858. They were very close, but eventually they separated around *the question of angels.* Wallace was convinced that guiding intelligences or angels would be necessary to explain the developments of the universe, and that natural selection did not fully account for the immense creativity in nature that occurred over a very limited time period. Darwin's position, however, resulted in "a gloomy materialism which now pervades the thinking of neo-Darwinism," including the notion that "the universe has no meaning or purpose," comments Sheldrake (24).

Aquinas was convinced that angels or spirits play an important role in bringing the prophetic imagination alive in people. He believed that angels learn exclusively by intuition and a lot of prophetic insight derives from intuition. "The divine enlightenments and revelations are conveyed from God to humans by the angels. . . . Prophetic revelation which is conveyed by the ministry of the angels, is said to be divine [revelations]" (89). Dreams often play a part in the process of waking prophets up, and Aquinas recognized that explicitly.

This is why he insisted that "angels carry thoughts from prophet to prophet." The image I get from this observation is that of bumblebees carrying pollen from flower to flower.

Since Aquinas teaches that angels learn exclusively by intuition—they don't need schools, teachers, or books—it follows that when we become more in touch with our intuition or mysticism, it is very likely that we will come into contact with angels. As we mature into our mystical brain you can expect more encounters with angels. Einstein says that intuition and deep feeling are the same thing. Angels "hitchhike" on the highway of intuition. After all, the word "muse"—from which we get "music" and "museum"—refers to those angels that accompany us during our most creative times. Many artists encounter angels or spirits in their creative moments. It wouldn't hurt to invite angels into one's life when one is busy solving problems or creating art.

Aquinas tells us that "angels are always announcers of divine silence" (91). Silence is surely one of the deep ways into the human heart and into divine mysteries, and it is integral to many forms of meditation in both the east and the west. But Aquinas gives credit to angels for bringing silence alive.

He is also being somewhat paradoxical in calling angels "announcers of divine silence." Isn't announcing always an act of speaking? Not necessarily, Aquinas clarifies—not when it comes to the divine silence, which is so deep and speaks to us deep to deep, depth to depth, heart to heart.

But Aquinas also says that the angels don't stop with the announcing; they also assist us *to understand and interpret the divine silence* derived from the divine mystery. "It is necessary after something is announced to someone that they understand the announcement. In addition, therefore, because we can understand by the intellect the things that are announced to us through the angels, they themselves by the brightness of their own light help our intellect grasp the secrets of God" (94).

According to Aquinas, "angels cannot help loving, by force of nature. The will of angels is by nature loving" (102). The universe, inhabited by angels, is neither impersonal nor neutral. There is a lot of love going on. Angels are compassionate beings that care and love. Sheldrake comments again: "The gravitational field unifies the whole universe. Like love, it is unifying by its nature. But we usually think of gravitational attraction as a completely unconscious process. To introduce this element of consciousness goes far beyond the field concept of contemporary science" (100).

We have metaphors that connect gravity and love, such as "falling in love." It is good to know that we are loved by cosmic forces like angels, since there are times when human love fails us.

Lorna Byrne, an Irish peasant woman who has been experiencing angels ever since she was two years old, says that today "there are many unemployed angels in the world." They are here because "God knows how much trouble humans are in today and is sending many angels to earth to assist us. But no one is asking them for help." Thus, unemployment reigns among the angelic host.

Is it time to ask them for help once more?

There is a

        Double

                Resurrection

29. There is a double Resurrection.*

Thomas Aquinas surprises us when he teaches that there are two resurrections: The first is waking up within this lifetime. And he implies that if we do this correctly, we need not worry about the second.

I have not heard such a teaching in any Christian writer before. Aquinas explains the "first resurrection" this way: "First, let us try to rise spiritually from the soul's death, brought on by our sins, to that life of justice obtained through penitence: 'Rise, you who sleep, and rise from the dead; and Christ shall enlighten you' (Eph 5:14). This is the first resurrection: 'blessed and holy is one who has part in the first resurrection' (John 20:6).'"

Being asleep is a kind of death from which we need to rise up and resurrect. The first resurrection is about Waking Up. He cites Paul's letter to the Romans: "'As Christ is risen from the dead by the glory of the Father, so we also must walk in newness of life' (Rom 6:4). The new life is the life of justice renewing the soul and leading it to the life of glory."

How prevalent is sleepfulness? Kabir, the fifteenth-century Indian mystic, tells us: "You have been sleeping for millions and millions of years. Why not wake up

---

* *Sheer Joy*, 361.

this morning?" Aquinas invokes the apostle Paul with an image found in Isaiah 60:1: "'Arise, be enlightened, O Jerusalem; for your light is come, and the glory of the Lord is risen upon you. 'Rise from a neglect of good works, you who sleep. 'How long will you sleep, O sluggard?' (Prov. 6:9). 'Shall he that sleep rise again no more?' (Ps 41:9)."

Says Aquinas: "There is a double resurrection, one of the body, when the soul rejoins body, the other spiritual, when soul reunited to God. Christ's bodily resurrection produces both in us—though he himself never rose again spiritually, for he had never been separated from God." Our being asleep is being separated from God. It is also succumbing to *acedia,* the capital sin often translated as *sloth* but with a far richer meaning that includes depression, despair, passivity, boredom—and also couchpotatoitis. Aquinas defines acedia as "the lack of energy to begin new things." We find it everywhere today, it is a "sign of our times," and that is why we created a new word for it—namely, couchpotatoitis.

Its cure is Waking Up. But how does that happen? Aquinas offers the medicine when he observes that zeal comes from an intense experience of love or beauty or goodness (114). Yes, beauty and falling in love are the cure for acedia and being asleep. The Via Positiva requires our attention. I wrote in my book *Liberating*

Gifts for the Peoples of the Earth of the need to fall in love at least three times per day. Of course, such falling in love is not into an anthropocentric kind of love—it is falling in love with creation itself and its many expressions of beauty and of the divine. Why not fall in love with wild flowers and elephants and trees and flowers, as well as music and poetry and pottery and films and the rest?

When we fall in love with life, we live this life fully as both mystics and prophets. Then we are awake and risen and have undergone our first resurrection. Upon dying, then, the second resurrection takes care of itself.

Aquinas believes that Christ explicitly calls us to both the first and second resurrection: "Our Lord promises both resurrections, for he says: 'Amen, Amen, I say to you that the hour is coming, and now is, when the dead shall hear the voice of the Son of God and they that hear shall live.' And this seems to pertain to the spiritual resurrection of souls. . . . But later, it is the bodily resurrection he expresses, saying: 'The hour is coming when all that are in the graves shall hear the voice of the Son of God' (John 5:25, 28). For, clearly souls are not in the graves, but bodies. Therefore, this foretells the bodily resurrection."

Nor is resurrection restricted to believers, but a "new creation "and a "common resurrection" happens to all and has already begun. "On that day on which the resurrection took place a kind of new creation, as it were, began. As the psalmist says 'Send forth your Spirit, and they will be created, and you will renew the face of the earth' (104:30). And as Galatians puts it: 'In Christ Jesus neither does circumcision nor uncircumcision have any value, but a new creation does. . . . The life of the risen Christ is spread to all humanity in common resurrection. Christ's resurrection is the cause of newness of life which comes through grace or justice (6:15)". As humans awaken, a new creation emerges.

God is
a Fountain of
Total Beauty,
the most beautiful
and the superbeautiful.

30. God is a Fountain of Total Beauty, the most beautiful and the superbeautiful.*

The idea that God is Beauty was totally lost in modern philosophy and, I'm sorry to say, in modern theology as well. Descartes, one of the founding fathers of modern philosophy, including its approach to education, offers an entire philosophy with little attention to aesthetics. Sadly, many theologians followed suit. One wonders how much of the ecological crisis staring us in the face today is traceable to our eliminating the premodern understanding of God as Beauty.

Aquinas was thoroughly marinated in the theological concept of God as Beauty. He brings this premodern wisdom to our spiritually-starving postmodern times. Following are some of his teachings on this important subject. "God is 'always' and uniformly beautiful. . . . God is a fountain of total beauty. The beautiful is said to be from God as a cause. From this beautiful One beauty comes to be in all beings, for brightness comes from a consideration of beauty. But all beauty, through which a thing is able to be, is a kind of participation of the divine brightness."

Much of the prayer of the Navajo people in America is built around beauty. One such prayer goes like this:

---

* *Sheer Joy*, 105, 106.

"I walk with beauty before me; I walk with beauty behind me; I walk with beauty above me; I walk with beauty below me; I walk with beauty all around me; your world is so beautiful, O God." Aquinas would be very comfortable with this kind of prayer; it fits a premodern mindset perfectly.

Aquinas elaborates on his linking of divinity and beauty when he declares: "God, who is supersubstantial beauty, is called beauty because God bestows beauty on all created beings." Key to beauty for Aquinas is harmony, brightness, and proportion.

When he speaks of "brightness," he is speaking of *doxa*, glory, or, as I have pointed out, the Cosmic Christ that is present in all beings. "God puts into creatures, along with a kind of 'sheen,' a reflection of God's own luminous 'ray,' which is the fountain of all light." The Cosmic Christ is that "luminous ray."

Significantly, contemporary science tells us that photons or light waves exist in every atom in the universe.

Aquinas insists that "the beautiful is God" and that all things operate for the sake of the beautiful just as all things operate for the sake of the good. "The beautiful, which is God, is the end of all like the final cause of all things. For all things have been made in order that they imitate the divine beauty in whatever way possible." We exist to imitate the divine beauty. One is reminded of the observation by Gustav Mahler who said that "all creation adorns itself continually for God. Everyone therefore has only one duty, to be as beautiful as possible in every way in the eyes of God and man. Ugliness is an insult to God."[38]

Do goodness and beauty differ? Aquinas believes that "the good and the beautiful are the same" though "beauty adds to goodness a relation to the cognitive faculty." The distinction lies in this: That "the 'good' simply pleases the appetite, while the 'beautiful' is something pleasant to apprehend. The senses most drawn to the beautiful are the most cognitive ones, such as sight and hearing, for we speak of beautiful sights and beautiful sounds." Sight and hearing most feed the intellect and imagination.

Years ago I was awakened to the moral dimension that beauty arouses when a Greek Orthodox theologian said to me: "In our tradition, the bottom line for determining the right and wrong of an action is this: 'Is what I am doing, is what we are doing, beautiful or not?'" Maybe this is one reason that the Greek Orthodox Church is far ahead of the Western church in responding to the ecological crisis.

Aquinas steers us back to honoring the Via Positiva. We are to treat beauty *with reverence*, he writes (and reverence is part of what is aroused by awe, wonder, and beauty in the Via Positiva). We are to do two things with beauty he says: (1) hold beauty in reverence, and (2) share beauty, rendering it conspicuous. "In addition to holding both beautiful things and good things in reverence, it is necessary for good things to be conspicuous, because to be conspicuous pertains to the nature of beauty." Yes! Beauty wants to put itself out there. The sun shines everywhere.

All beauty yearns to be conspicuous.

Christ is
a dew for cooling;
rain for making fruitful;
a seed for bringing forth
the fruit of justice.

31. Christ is a dew for cooling; rain for making fruitful; a seed for bringing forth the fruit of justice.*

Who is Christ for Thomas Aquinas? I don't know about you, reader, but I get tired hearing one title for Jesus repeated over and over, such as "Jesus is my Lord and Savior." How many other titles or images of Jesus might be out there?

Aquinas offers an amazing array of titles for Jesus, all of which are fruitful and interesting. Our intelligence can be easily insulted by watering down his presence and teachings to just a few names. The conduits to mystery and wisdom that Jesus unleashed are multiple, rich and varied. Let us consider some names Aquinas presents for our meditation and imitation.

Aquinas sees Christ as the Word who is "the beauty conceived in the heart of the Father." Christ harbors a "fourfold beauty" that includes the divine beauty or form of God, "the beauty of justice and truth," and the beauty of honest conversation.

Aquinas speaks of the *wetness* of Christ when he says "Christ is a dew for cooling; rain for making fruitful; a seed for bringing forth fruit." And "the fruit spoken of is justice," which derives from Christ in three

---

* *Sheer Joy*, 367.

179

ways: "by his labor, by his speaking and teaching, and as a gift he has given out."

The fruit Jesus teaches is justice for "he has fulfilled justice by his labor, as in Matthew 3: 'Thus it is fitting for us to fulfill all justice.' He has taught justice in his speaking, as in Isaiah 63: 'I who announce justice, and am a defender with power to save.' And he gave justice as a gift, as in 1 Corinthians 1: "He has been made wisdom and holiness and justice for us.'"

By his resurrection, Christ "raised us up first as a victor in order to free his captive. Second, like a doctor to heal the sick. Third, like a lawyer to acquit a defendant. Fourth, like a brave person who defends the weak. Fifth, as a husband who takes pleasure with his spouse as it says in Hosea 2: 'I will wed myself to you in justice and in faith.'"

Furthermore, Christ is a teacher—indeed "Christ alone is the master teaching within each of us." We are told that "he teaches the dignity of human nature . . . and the full participation in Divinity, which is truly humanity's happiness and the goal of human life" (162).

He is a "teacher of wisdom." In addition, he is "wisdom personified of whom it is written, 'I, wisdom, have poured forth rivers. . . .' But now, 'the depths of the rivers he has searched, and the hidden things he has brought to light' (Job 28:11)." Christ is a teacher because he is wisdom incarnate. "Insofar as he is the wisdom of God, he teaches all people, and therefore his disciples called him 'Lord,' as in John 6:69, 'Lord, to whom shall we go?' and also teacher, as in John 4:51. Rightly so, for he is the one Lord creating and re-creating."

What does it mean to call Christ "Wisdom"? "This is what the highest wisdom does: it manifests the hidden truth of Divinity; it produces the works of creation, and furthermore restores them at need; it brings them to the completion of achieving their own proper and perfect purpose." Notice that "restoration," or what some call "redemption," is only one of three works of Wisdom, including revealing divine mysteries and creating and bringing things to their full purpose. Aquinas also combines "creating" and "restoring"—he does not allow "redemption" to stand alone or to be isolated and cut off from the work of creation. How paltry it is of some versions of Christianity to reduce the entire message to only one-fourth of the work of wisdom!

Aquinas also speaks of the Cosmic Christ. "God knows and makes creatures. Thus the Word is expressive of God the Creator; yet it is both expressive and creative of the universe." Indeed, "The formation of everything is attributed to the Word; thus the psalmist says: 'The skies have been formed by the word of the Lord' (Ps 33)." Wisdom is cosmic, and the Cosmic Christ is cosmic wisdom. "One of divine wisdom's functions is to create. . . . It is Wisdom in person who speaks: 'I was with him forming all things' (Prov 8:30). So we think of the Son when calling the image of God invisible and the pattern to which all things are made. 'The first-born of every creature, for in him were all things created in heaven and on earth' (Col 1:15-16). Since all things were made through him' (John 1:3) rightly do we think of the Son when it is written, 'I am like a stream flowing from the waters of a great river.'" It is striking how in this one paragraph Aquinas gathers so many biblical references to the Cosmic Christ taken from John's gospel, Colossians, and wisdom literature such as the books of Psalms, Proverbs, and Wisdom.

Instead of "redemption," Aquinas uses the term *restoration and repairing* when he declares: "The one who makes a thing is the one who can repair it, and so the restoration of creation is the third function of wisdom: 'by wisdom were they healed' (Wis 9:19). This especially was the work of the Son, who was made human in order to change the very state of our nature and restore everything human: 'Through him reconciling all things unto himself, both what is on earth and what is in heaven' (Col 1:20)." To speak of "restore everything human" is a powerful statement about returning to our deepest humility.

In calling Christ the "splendor of God's glory," Aquinas again names the Cosmic Christ. He tells us that Christ assumed at the transfiguration event "the clarity of glory as to its essence." He was transfigured "in order to show human beings his glory and to rouse them to a desire for it themselves."

Christ's "teachings are water," Aquinas says, because they are abundant; they make things cool, 'cold water for the thirsty soul' (Prov 25); they make fruitful; they move quickly and "because it shapes itself for individuals, as Proverbs puts it (5): 'Divide your waters into channels' (Prov 5)."

For Aquinas "Christ is a book. A book is an instrument in which there are conceptions of the heart—but in Christ there are conceptions of the divine intellect. Colossians says: 'In him are hidden all the treasures of the wisdom and knowledge of God' (Col 2). The heading of the book is God the Creator" (371–72).

Christ rouses us to action and is our life. "Some call that by which they are roused to activity their 'life.' Hunters, for example, call hunting their life, and friends their friend. So, Christ is our life, because the whole principle of our life and activity is Christ."

Christ is God-with-us. "Isaiah says (7:2) that 'his name will be called Emmanuel,' that is, God-with-us, because Christ is with us in many ways" including, as a brother; as "a husband through the bonds of love"; as a shepherd, "through the solace of a maternal comfort"; as a savior, "through the help of protection. Jeremiah (30) says: 'So do not fear.' And like a leader." Notice again that the term "savior" is only one among several titles here and is defined here as protection.

The fourth function of divine wisdom is "the fostering of things to the fulfillment of their purpose. Otherwise, what is left but vanity . . .? Wisdom 'reaches from end to end mightily and orders all things sweetly' (Wis 8:1)" (376).

Christ is a warrior anointed with "an oil of boundless courage, like a fighter for the purpose of fighting. 2 Kings 1 says: 'How has the shield of the brave been cast down, the shield of Saul and Jonathan, as if it had not been anointed with oil?'" The warrior and prophet are similar archetypes, and Aquinas sees Jesus as a prophet when he says "Christ was a prophet—and the greatest of the prophets." This is clear from "'The Lord your God will raise up a prophet among you, from your nation and your brothers; he will be like me. You will listen to him' (Deut 18:15). This text is referred to Christ. The greatest of the prophets is none other than Christ" (446–47).

What are some implications of recognizing Christ

as prophet? "It is characteristic of prophets to reveal what is not present but hidden."

Because Christ is also Wisdom incarnate, he is more than a prophet: "Although Christ was a prophet, he was more than a prophet because he produces prophets: 'Wisdom produces friends of God and prophets' (Wis 7:27)." To Aquinas Christ has broken down barriers between peoples, including Jews and Gentiles, and Aquinas foresees a vision of harmony and peace among all people, a new humanity. "Christ's coming has broken down the old barrier of damnation. The entire human race is now more open to receive grace than before. . . . Now the Gospel has been preached and all is set for every imperfection of our humanity to be cleared away" (443). He imagines a very rich future for the human race.

Christ is also "compassion" (see chapter 21). And Christ is Light (141).

In addition, Christ is a doctor. "Christ was given to us in the role of a doctor." And "as a watchman." And "as a defender." As a shepherd, "as in Ezekiel 34: 'And I will raise up for them a shepherd, to feed them.'" He is also called a "gardener." In addition, he gives us an "example of his labor," which we find in "the food of travelers; the price of redemption; the reward of recompense" (381).

And "Christ is like a mother" (382). It is "Christ who brings us to glory, Christ who brings to birth the church's faithful: 'Shall not I that make others to bring forth children myself bring forth, says the Lord; shall I, that give birth to others be barren, says the Lord your God?' (Isa 66:9)" (382).

I count in this chapter *thirty-four names* that Thomas Aquinas has offered for Christ. Aren't those names much more interesting and varied, rich and enticing, than just "lord and savior"? Don't these *arouse* (Aquinas's word) the imagination, mind, and heart to do good things in imitation of him and in his name? Don't they awaken us to develop our own names for Jesus and his work, to let our minds wander and create and co-create?

It is impossible
that anyone
hide the words of God,
when their heart
is inflamed by love.

Conclusion

The Tao of Fierce Wisdom by Thomas Aquinas

We have been considering the essence of Aquinas's teachings about our spiritual journey toward wisdom, justice, and compassion. A journey that takes us away from dullness, indifference, and, in his words, folly. "Folly implies apathy in the heart and dullness in the senses," he writes, "for *sapiens* (wise) as Isidore says 'is so named from *sapor* (savor), because just as the taste is quick to distinguish between savors of meats, so too a wise person is quick in discerning things and causes.' Thus it is clear that folly is opposed to wisdom as its contrary . . . the fool has the sense, though dulled, whereas the wise person has the sense acute and penetrating."

Yet overcoming apathy in the heart and dullness in the senses the goal is not just about awareness but also action. For "Wisdom is able to direct us not only in contemplation but also in action" (378). For Aquinas "prayer consists in two things: namely, in the interior action of the heart, and in exterior works" (263). This corresponds exactly to my teaching on prayer as a "radical response to life," which includes our mysticism (the Via Positiva and Via Negativa) and our prophecy (the

Via Creativa and Via Transformativa).[39] It is all the work of the Spirit who "ennobles us and makes us leaders" (265). Indeed, it is "the same Holy Spirit that inspired the prophets and the authors of Sacred Scripture that moved the saints to work. For, as 2 Peter (1:21) says: 'The holy ones of God have spoken inspired by the Holy Spirit.'"

The work is both inner and outer, mystical and prophetic. "The apostles, who are the chiefs and leaders of Christian wisdom and were motivated every day by truth, *witnessed as is appropriate, not only in word but also in work*" (266).

And he urges fire in the heart. "It is impossible that anyone hide the words of God when their heart is inflamed by love. . . . But the cause of one's excitement is the meditation on divine things; whence the psalmist says: 'And the fire burned in my meditation.'" He offers this advice: "If you wish to arrive at spiritual things your heart must be inflamed with love of God. The effect of the excitement is that one who preferred to be silent is moved to speak. . . . Acts (2) says: 'All were filled with the Holy Spirit, and they began to speak'" (267).

To conclude this journey with Aquinas, I choose to present his words in a poetic modality much like the *Tao Te Ching*. Here we summarize his teachings in his own words, words that constitute the chapter titles to this book, arranged in poetic form. As they so deserve.

The Tao of Fierce Wisdom by Thomas Aquinas

The experience of God
must not be restricted
    to the few
    or to the old.
"They shall be drunk
      on the beauty
       of thy house,"
         that is, the universe.

Revelation comes
        in two volumes:
        Nature
        and the Bible.
The greatness of the human person
consists in this:
that we are
capable of the universe.
A mistake about nature
      results in
      a mistake about God.

Sheer Joy is God's
      and this demands
      companionship.

Joy
is the human's
> *noblest act.*
Religion is
supreme thankfulness
or gratitude.
The first and primary meaning
of salvation
is this:
> *To preserve things*
> > *in the good.*
The same Spirit
who hovered over the waters
at the beginning of creation
hovers over the mind
of the artist
at work.
We ought to cherish the body
and celebrate
the wonderful communion
of body and soul.

Every truth without exception—
—and whoever may utter it—
is from the Holy Spirit.
Revelation

has been made
to many pagans.
The old pagan virtues
were from God.

Every being
is a name for God;
and no being
is a name for God.
We are united
to God
as to One Unknown.
The greatest accomplishment
of the human mind
is to know
that it does not know
who God is.

The first requirement, then,
for the contemplation of wisdom,
is that we should take complete possession
of our minds
before anything else does.

It is a great thing
to do miracles.

Matthew Fox

But it is a greater thing
to live virtuously.
The proper objects
of the heart
are truth
and justice.
The vision of God
is arrived at
through Justice.

Compassion is the fire
that Jesus came
to set on the earth.
Conscience is
more to be obeyed
than authority imposed from
the outside.
The prophet's mind is moved
not only to apprehend something,
but also
to speak
or to do something.
A trustworthy person is angry
at the right people,
for the right reasons,
expresses it in the appropriate manner

and for an appropriate
length of time.
Playfulness
or Fun
is a Virtue.
It pertains to Magnanimity
to have
a great soul.
Angels carry thoughts
from prophet
to prophet.

There is
a double
Resurrection.
God is
a fountain
of total Beauty,
the most beautiful
and the superbeautiful.
Christ is
a dew for cooling;
rain for making fruitful;
a seed
for bringing forth the fruit of justice.
It is impossible

that anyone
hide the words of God,
when their heart
is inflamed by love.

Amen.

Afterword

Jerry Maynard, OMM

While reading *The Tao of Thomas Aquinas*, I found myself with an overwhelming feeling of joy and, when finished, had a very profound sense of being affirmed. My soul found familiar echoes within Aquinas's words of wisdom and the exegesis composed by the Rev. Dr. Matthew Fox. There were several instances, however, where I wondered: Is this real? Could the messages in this book be too good to be true? Perhaps you relate to my questions on some level, especially as my reasoning is fleshed out.

First off, let us talk about joy. As we have read, Thomas Aquinas has profound truths to share about the nature of joy—from joy being a necessary "companion" (chaps 6, 37) to joy being the "noblest act" (chaps 7, 40). One of the reasons why I personally felt an extensive amount of joy while reading was due to the fact that I felt a great saint (whose work I have enjoyed reading in the past) was speaking directly to me in my current context—a reality that proves Aquinas speaks wisdom for our times.

I was not only experiencing euphoria, however, but a deep sense of resonance with the sentiments being expressed: a shared experience of discovering these beautiful truths in my own life. I can testify that I have been able to embody many of the realities that Aquinas describes. Matthew Fox, in chapter 6 states, "joy begs for sharing" (chaps 6, 37), and I would add that joy motivates us to share not just mere commonalities but also the universal realities of being human—in a word, solidarity. Joy motivates us to live in solidarity with the human family.

In my life, I have experienced moments of intense joy that manifested while doing the work of justice. For example, I was part of a delegation of activists and faith leaders who spent three days in Nogales, Arizona, for the Encuentro Frontera (Border Encounter) sponsored by the School of the Americas Watch (SOAW). On the first full day, we gathered to have a march for brown families, and, during that march, I carried a sign saying, "You are welcome here." When our group split (some went into Mexico) I stayed on the US side to wave to the families that gathered along the wall. My sign was in Spanish, and when I would pass by, many people stopped and asked if they could take a picture of my sign. One woman told me (in what little English she knew) that she felt "blessed to know people in America cared about her," and then she gave me an *abrazo* (hug) through the wall.

Another instance where I encountered an authentic experience of joy was when I was in downtown Houston with my fellow antihomelessness activists passing out free food. We are part of an international decentralized movement called "Food Not Bombs." While setting up on this particularly cold night a young boy (maybe eight years of age) asked me what we were giving out that night. I said soup. It was not clear to me whether this child had not eaten in days, or whether he was just the biggest fan of soup in all of humanity, but when I said the word "soup" his entire face just lit up like a light bulb!

Later that same night, while finishing up my time visiting with people, I began to gather myself in order to head home (I was one of the last volunteers to leave this night). At some point I looked up after answering a text message and was amazed to see a group of unhoused friends laughing, running around, enjoying the fact that they had a full belly. In that moment, as I realized that this is what Jesus meant when he said "your kingdom come . . . on earth as it is in heaven," the words of Jesuit priest, theologian, and scientist Pierre Teilhard de Chardin popped into my head: "Joy is the infallible sign of the presence of God." Watching this merriment was like being granted a glimpsed into the possibility of what communion really means: for that night, our soup and our presence was the life force that liberated weary bodies.

When we invest in one another, when we choose to affirm each other by being in solidarity with the most vulnerable of our world, we are exposed to the deep mystery of communion, and we may discover what St. Augustine of Hippo meant when he said: "The glory of God is a [human being] fully alive." Speaking of affirming, let us talk about that next.

As I mentioned in the beginning, I experienced a deep sense of being affirmed while reading through this book on Thomas Aquinas. Why was this, I wondered—and then I realized that through the words of Aquinas, my generation *(millennials)* was being granted permission (by a saint!) not only to claim our rightful place as prophets but also to embrace wholeheartedly our identities as the beloved of God.

Aquinas—whether he knew it or he did not know it centuries ago when writing down these teachings—testifies to the life expressions of many young adults all over this world who have been acting upon the inner tug of Spirit to move forward in daring to build a radically different world where justice is the foundation, elitism is no more, and tenderness is our culture.

One of my favorite passages in this book, one that made me want to run a marathon because I was so energized by it, is found in the first chapter, where Rev. Dr. Fox quotes Aquinas:

> Youth is the cause of hope on these three counts, namely because the object of hope is future, is difficult, and is possible. For the young live in the future and not in the past; they are not lost in memories but full of confidence.

Aquinas goes on:

> Second, their warmth of nature, high spirits, and expansive heart emboldens them to reach out to difficult projects; therefore they are mettlesome and of good hope.

The quote continues, of course, but I just want to highlight the phrases "expansive heart" and "they are mettlesome and of good hope." I love this! O, what truth! When I first read these lines, I wanted to cry tears of joy because I felt like my life was being given the proper praise it was due.

Lastly, Aquinas writes, "Third, they have not been thwarted in their plans, and their lack of experience encourages them to think that where there's a will there's a way." I would testify that young adults do not "lack experience," but rather they have different experiences that are unique to the very new issues of our times. This last line, however, denotes the inherent "overcomer" spirit that I think is inherently present among a lot of young adults who refuse to give up and insist upon being treated justly.

This beautiful affirmation from Thomas Aquinas sets us up for realizing that we must learn to delight in one another. Aquinas says, "For delight is the perfection of happiness, as beauty is that of youth" (*Sheer Joy*, 505).

Also in chapter 1, Matthew and Aquinas affirm what I tell others from time to time: "He encourages all to *get a life*, an *inner* life, and start paying attention to our experiences of beauty and truth, of oneness and oneing, in short to value our mystical experiences and make them the basis of our consciences, our choices, our values, our work, and our goals" (chaps 1, 18).

As I mentioned before, it is clear that Thomas Aquinas is praising those of us who are engaging in living consciously and with keen attention towards how our interior lives are influencing our exterior world. The process of developing an inner life and grappling with what is found in the deepest parts of our being is often neglected or undernourished by socially engaged people. This is why, as an activist priest, I do my best to assist in curating space where this sacred work can be done. This leads me, however, to those two pesky questions that kept recurring to me while reading this book—namely, *is this true* and *could the messages in this book be too good to be true*?

Those of us who are young adults, particularly queer black and brown young adults who may have differing neurological and/or physical abilities, are sadly accustomed to being targeted, abused, and thrown out by sacred institutions.

An air of suspicion from ecclesial institutions, who value respectability rather than justice, forces those who find themselves on the negative (and often violent) side of religiosity to cultivate a deep distrust, which prevents the ability to cultivate joy, and then completely smother any possibility for affirmation.

For me, this distrust is very real, and I relate in many ways to individuals who have been wounded by institutional religion. As a young person and ordained faith leader with differing physical abilities, I often find that seeking protection is something I consciously engage in on a daily basis—whether physical protection by seeking out spaces where my visual impairment or neurological difference will not keep me from full participation, or organizational protection so that there is some barrier between myself and the cruelty of others.

This reality of needing protection is very tangible for members of a variety of targeted communities who have historically been scapegoated, or even murdered, because the system dehumanized the community. (The Black Panthers are a great example of a community that was scapegoated and dehumanized.) Being abandoned by people who claim to be on our side can make us start to question (as I do), all that is brought before us.

From this understanding, I think it is clear why the question of "is this real" might arise. The words of Thomas Aquinas are a blessing of respite from constantly wondering whether we will be loved, whether we will be included, or whether we will need to pick up our things and go because we will not be wanted. These questions and internal struggles are direct by-products of a system inherently designed to deny us our rights to dignity, integrity, and ownership of our lived experiences. But, as we see, Aquinas encourages us to reclaim our dignity and integrity by insisting on paying attention to our lived experiences and doing the work of resisting all that denies us our experiences.

In my work as an activist and community organizer, I often find those of us who show up regularly—and dare to draw deep upon our courage to do this very difficult work of justicemaking—get burned so frequently that we lose our balance. Among changemakers, burnout, coupled with fatigue caused by repression, usually causes people to quit. I have also found that one of the ways ongoing oppression takes its toll is through the recurring idea that we do not "deserve" to be a part of the vastness of life. Feeling like we are not worthy, and then being regularly told by institutions that we *are* not worthy, is brutal beyond words.

There are also those of us who actively resist these lies by living our truths daily but often succumbing to crippling doubt that makes us question our very identity. This is most frequently called *imposter syndrome*—the belief that you are a fraud. These realities, which not only I but many others deal with also in our lives, are intense and often make activists very edgy.

But I find hope in chapter 1, where Matthew quotes a line in which it is clear that Aquinas encourages us to use self-love as the antidote to this regularly occurring struggle of self-doubt. Aquinas says, "Self-love is the form and root of all friendship. To know and appreciate your own worth is no sin" (*Sheer Joy*, 99). Indeed, knowing your own self-worth is not a sin but an act of revolution!

In my opinion, one of the greatest sins of our world is the idea that we have the authority to decide who is worthy of being made in the image and likeness of the divine. As the great Dutch spiritual writer and Catholic priest Henri Nouwen used to say, "We are the beloved [children] of God," and he is absolutely correct. It is our constant duty to reclaim the core of our identity: belovedness—or, as Matthew would say, our "original blessing."

Do you agree, or do you think this is too good to be true?

To be completely honest, even though I have read many works by Thomas Aquinas and know his theology and spirituality, I still doubted the wisdom I was reading and even thought to myself, "This is all just a gimmick." But then I thought "So what?!" If this is too good to be true, then that means I must reevaluate my understanding of truth. As I was reflecting on various passages, an epiphany occurred that opened my eyes. If the messages of Thomas Aquinas present here are "too good to be true" *then that is exactly why I need them*— because they are coming from a place of goodness that reflects back to me, like a mirror, my own innate goodness. After this realization, I noticed the title of chapter 9: "The first and primary meaning of salvation is this: To preserve things in the good." The three words that stood out to me were *salvation*, *preserve*, and *good*.

The idea that salvation was the act of "preserving all things in the good" was absolutely electrifying to me! At a workshop on faith-based community organizing, I once stated that I believed our duty as faith leaders was less about saving souls and more about liberating bodies. Reading this quote from Aquinas makes me feel like he is seconding what I said, clarifying it by explaining that "liberating bodies" is to preserve them in goodness—namely, to be sure that people can eat, drink, have healthcare, and receive education.

Who knew that Thomas Aquinas, a medieval theologian and philosopher, was such a revolutionary?! Can we also dare to dwell in our innate goodness and demand that we be treated as the beloved children of God?

Our marching orders are clear, and the path has been set for us. We do not have the luxury of time to allow external forces to keep us from giving birth to new realities of global justice and cosmic oneness. We must embrace the beautiful wisdom in this book and get to work!

Thomas Aquinas, like many sages and prophets, has often been ignored to the point that his life becomes but a footnote in history, or his message is watered down to the point that the potency of his words is drowned out of existence. However, in this timely work, Rev. Dr. Matthew Fox has revived Aquinas for our time and given him a framework that allows all of us to recognize that this message is the instrument that will give our weary world a new song of liberation.

I would like to leave you with these words from the queer, black feminist and prophet Audre Lorde. May they charge you up with the power to become fierce lovers of truth, perpetrators of peace, and preachers of justice: "It is not difference which immobilizes us, but silence; and there are so many silences to be broken."[40]

Acknowledgements

I am in debt to many teachers for leading me to the well of Thomas Aquinas, beginning with a Dominican priest in my home parish when I was fifteen years old and extending to multiple Dominican professors at Aquinas Institute of Philosophy and Theology, including Father James Weisheipl, OP, and many more. To Father M.-D. Chenu, OP, for his brilliant writings, challenging and enthusiastic classes, and sustained encouragement through the years. To Josef Pieper and to G. K. Chesterton. To Meister Eckhart, who stands on Aquinas's shoulders and has led me on many deep adventures. And to Fiona Hallowell and Dover Publications for the new publication of my *Sheer Joy* book, with special mention of Father Bede Griffiths, who gave me critical feedback and upgraded my translations to the Queen's English and wrote the afterword, and to Rupert Sheldrake, who wrote the foreword and who reminds me, along with Thomas Berry and Brian Swimme, of the importance of Aquinas in the history of science. Thank you.

Thank you to artist Ullrrich Javier Garcia Lemus for the painting that graces the cover of this edition, and to J. Andrew Edwards for his copyediting and suggestions that improved the current manuscript. And a special shout-out to Ilia Delio and Jerry Maynard for their insightful foreword and afterword, respectively. And to Dennis Edwards, Ron Tuazon, and Mara for their daily support. To Hailee Pavey for her beautiful cover designs.

To iUniverse publishers and to Jill Angelo and Andrew Harvey who encouraged me to work with these publishers. Thank you to Aileen Myers and Vinnia Alvarez of iUniverse for their production help and coaching.

To my fellow workers with dailymeditationswithmatthewfox.org including Phila Hoopes, Richard Reich, Mary Plaster, Ellyn Kennedy.

To Aaron Stern and his coworkers at the Academy for the Love of Learning, for their support and encouragement. And to those who took the time to read an advance version of the manuscript and create the blurbs that are found in the front pages. Thank you!

Sources

As indicated in my introduction, all the Aquinas citations are taken from Matthew Fox, *Sheer Joy: Conversations with Thomas Aquinas on Creation Spirituality.* One can go there to find the references to Aquinas's works. The following lists the Latin sources from which I have culled his words:

Commentary on Aristotle's De Anima
Commentary on Denys the Areopagite's De divinis nominibus
Commentary on Aristotle's Ethics
Commentary on Aristotle's Metaphysics
Commentary on Aristotle's Politics
Commentary on Peter Lombard's Books of Sentences
Commentary on Job
Commentary on the Psalms
Commentary on Isaiah
Commentary on Jeremiah
Commentary on the Book of Lamentations
Commentary on the Gospel of Matthew
Commentary on the Gospel of John
Commentary on the Letter to the Romans
Commentary on the First Letter to the Corinthians
Commentary on the Letter to the Ephesians

Matthew Fox

Commentary on the Letter to the Philippians
Commentary on the Letter to the Colossians
Commentary on the Letter to the Hebrews
Commentary on the Letter to the Thessalonians
Commentary on the Letter to Timothy
Compendium theologiae
De malo (On Evil)
De Potentia (On Power)
De Veritate (On Truth)
Questiones quodlibetales
Sermon on the Apostles Creed
Summa contra Gentiles
Summa theologiae

Notes

1   M.-D. Chenu, *Faith and Theology* (New York: Macmillan, 1968), 33.

2   Matthew Fox, *Sheer Joy: Conversations with Thomas Aquinas on Creation Spirituality* (Mineola, NY: Dover Publications, 2020), 466.

3   See Matthew Fox, "Meister Eckhart on the Four-Fold Path of a Creation-Centered Spirituality," in Matthew Fox, *Western Spirituality: Historical Roots, Ecumenical Routes* (Santa Fe, NM: 1981), 215–48. The Four Paths are developed further in Matthew Fox, *Original Blessing* (New York: Jeremy P. Tarcher, 2000).

4   Lao-Tzu, *Tao Te Ching: A New English Version*, trans. Stephen Mitchell (San Francisco: HarperSanFrancisco, 1988), no. 38.

5   Matthew Fox, *Passion for Creation: The Earth-Honoring Spirituality of Meister Eckhart* (Rochester, VT: Inner Traditions, 2000), 312.

6   Abraham Joshua Heschel, *Man Is Not Alone: A Philosophy of Religion* (New York: Farrar, Straus, and Young, 1951), 58.

7   Abraham Joshua Heschel, *I Asked for Wonder* (New York: Crossroad, 1987), 2–3.

8   Qtd. in William Hermanns, *Einstein and the Poet: In Search of the Cosmic Man* (Brookline Village, MA: Branden Press, 1983), 68.

9   See Matthew Fox, *The Reinvention of Work* (San Francisco: HarperSanFrancisco, 1994), 296-308.

10 Thomas Berry, *The Great Work: Our Way into the Future* (New York: Bell Tower, 1988), 166.

11 See Matthew Fox, *Original Blessing.*

12 Thomas Berry, *The Great Work: Our Way into the Future* (New York: Bell Tower, 1999).

13 Rosemary Radford Ruether, "Patristic Spirituality and the Experience of Women in the Early Church," in Matthew Fox, ed., *Western Spirituality*), 145.

14 Abraham Joshua Heschel, *The Prophets* (New York: Harper & Row, 1962), 258.

15 Claude Tresmontant, *A Study of Hebrew Thought* (New York: Desclée, 1960), 47, 100.

16 M. C. Richards, *Imagine Inventing Yellow: New and Selected Poems of M. C. Richards* (Barrytown, NY: Station Hill, 1991), 40–41.

17 Luisah Teish, *Jambalaya: The Natural Woman's Book of Personal Charms and Practical Rituals* (New York: HarperCollins, 1985).

18 I give a shout out also to Linda Neale, *The Power of Ceremony: Restoring the Sacred in Our Selves, Our Families, Our Communities* (Portland, OR: Eagle Spirit Press, 2011).

19 See Matthew Fox, *Naming the Unnameable: 89 Wonderful and Useful Names for God . . . Including the Unnameable God* (Pawcatuck, CT: Little Bound Books, 2018).

20 Estelle Frankel, *The Wisdom of Not Knowing: Discovering a Life of Wonder by Embracing Uncertainty* (Boulder, CO: Shambhala Publications, 2017), 1.

21 Cited in Hermanns, *Einstein and the Poet,* 69.

22 For his commentary on the Sermon on the Mount, *Sheer Joy,* pp. 502–14.

23 bell hooks, *All About Love* (New York: William Morrow, 2001), 33.

24 Hermanns, *Einstein and the Poet*, 135.

25 See https://www.heartmath.org/science.

26 See M.-D. Chenu, "Body and Body Politic in the Creation Spirituality of Thomas Aquinas," in Fox, ed., *Western Spirituality,* 215–48, for a substantive discussion on this important topic.

27 See Claudio Naranjo and Robert E. Ornstein, *On the Psychology of Meditation* (New York: Viking, 1972), 91. See also Matthew Fox, "Deep Ecumenism, Ecojustice, and Art as Meditation," in *Wrestling with the Prophets* (New York: Jeremy P. Tarcher, 1995), 215–42.

28 See Suzi Gablik, "Art for Earth's Sake," *Resurgence & Ecologist* 202 (September–October 2000). http://s3.amazonaws.com/arena-attachments/1537178/725d17 36d884a63002459f06519438c4.pdf?1514400517

29 See Matthew Fox, "On Desentimentalizing Spirituality," in *Wrestling with the Prophets*, 297–316.

30 See Matthew Fox, "Thomas Aquinas: Mystic and Prophet of the Environment," in *ibid.,* 105–14.

31 Martin Luther King Jr., *Why We Can't Wait* (New York: Signet, 2000), 93–94. He also cites St. Augustine, Martin Buber, and Paul Tillich in this section of his "Letter from Birmingham Jail."

32 Heschel, *The Prophets,* 258.

33 C. G. Jung, "Psychological Types," in *The Collected Works of C. G. Jung*, Bollingen Series 20 (Princeton, NJ: Princeton University Press, 1971), 6:§93.

34 See Matthew Fox, *Sins of the Spirit, Blessings of the Flesh: Transforming Evil in Soul and Society* (Berkeley, CA: North Atlantic Books, 2016).

35 Jorge Mario Bergoglio and Abraham Skorka, *On Heaven and Earth: Pope Francis on Faith, Family and the Church in the 21st Century* (New York: Image, 2013), 10.

36 See Frédéric Martel, *In the Closet in the Vatican: Power, Homosexuality, Hypocrisy* (London: Continuum, 2019), 26–32. See also my "Review of Frederic Martel's *In the Closet of the Vatican*," *Tikkun* (June 24, 2019): https://www.tikkun. org/review-of-frederic-martels-in-the-closet-of-the-vatican/.

37 See Fox, *Sins of the Spirit, Blessings of the Flesh*, 183–374, where I compare the seven capital sins with the seven chakras.

38 Cited in Alma Mahler, *Gustav Mahler: Memories and Letters* (Seattle: University of Washington Press, 1968), 168.

39 See Matthew Fox, *Prayer: A Radical Response to Life* (New York: Jeremy P. Tarcher, 2001), 49–116, and Fox, *The Reinvention of Work.*

40 Audre Lorde, *Sister Outsider: Essays and Speeches*, Crossing Press Feminist Series (New York: Crossing Press, 2007), 44.

About the Author

Matthew Fox is author of over thirty-five books on culture and spirituality, which have been translated into seventy-five languages and received many awards. In his books and teaching he has brought alive the much neglected Creation Spirituality tradition of the West. He lectures internationally and has created a pedagogy for spiritual learning experiences that have reached many thousands of persons through Mundelein College in Chicago, Holy Names College, and the University of Creation Spirituality, which he founded and led for nine years in Oakland, California, along with his pilot program, YELLAWE, for inner city youth.

For speaking out on women's rights, gay rights, and Native American rights, he was silenced for a year and later expelled from the Dominican Order under the papacies of John Paul II and Benedict XVI. He then joined the Episcopal Church to work with young people to create postmodern forms of ritual and worship known as the "Cosmic Mass" that incorporates dance, DJ, VJ, rap, and other postmodern art forms. He is co-founder of the Order of the Sacred Earth and, since Mother's Day 2019, has offered free daily meditations at dailymeditationswithmatthewfox.org.

Fox is a visiting scholar at the Academy for the Love of Learning in Santa Fe, New Mexico, and he heads an online certificate course in Creation Spirituality and Leadership at Global Ministries University as of March, 2020. He is a recipient of the Abbey Courage of Conscience Peace Award, whose other recipients include the Dalai Lama, Rosa Parks, Mother Teresa, Ernesto Cardinale, and Maya Angelou. Other awards include the Gandhi, King, Ikeda Community Builders Prize from Morehouse College, the Humanities Award of the Sufi International Association of Sufism, and the Tikkun Ethics Award. See www.matthewfox.org.

Books by Matthew Fox

Original Blessing

The Coming of the Cosmic Christ

A Spirituality Named Compassion

Order of the Sacred Earth: An Intergenerational Vision of Love and Action (with Skylar Wilson and Jennifer Listug)

Prayer: A Radical Response to Life

Creation Spirituality: Liberating Gifts for the Peoples of the Earth

Whee! We, Wee All the Way Home: Toward a Prophetic, Sensual Spirituality Western Spirituality: Historical Roots, Ecumenical Routes (edited)

Natural Grace (with Rupert Sheldrake)

The Physics of Angels (with Rupert Sheldrake)

Christian Mystics: 365 Readings and Meditations

Passion for Creation: Meister Eckhart's Earth-Based Spirituality

Meister Eckhart: A Mystic-Warrior for Our Times

Meditations with Meister Eckhart

Illuminations of Hildegard of Bingen

Hildegard of Bingen, A Saint for Our Times: Unleashing Her Power in the 21st Century

Hildegard of Bingen's Book of Divine Works, Songs and Letters

Matthew Fox

Sheer Joy: Conversations with Thomas Aquinas on Creation Spirituality

A Way to God: Thomas Merton's Creation Spirituality Journey

The Reinvention of Work: A New Vision of Livelihood for Our Times

Creativity: Where the Divine and the Human Meet

The Hidden Spirituality of Men: Ten Metaphors to Awaken the Sacred Masculine

The A.W.E Project: Reinventing Education, Reinventing the Human

Occupy Spirituality: A Radical Vision for a New Generation (with Adam Bucko)

Sins of the Spirit, Blessings of the Flesh: Transforming Evil in Soul and Society

Wrestling with the Prophets: Essays on Creations Spirituality and Everyday Life

The Pope's War: Why Ratzinger's Secret Crusade Has Imperiled the Church and What Can Be Saved

Confessions: The Making of a Post-Denominational Priest

One River, Many Wells: Wisdom Springing from Global Faiths

Religion USA: Culture and Religion by way of Time Magazine

A New Reformation

Letters to Pope Francis

Naming the Unnameable: 89 Wonderful and Useful Names for God...Including the Unnameable God

Stations of the Cosmic Christ (with Bishop Marc Andrus)

The Lotus & the Rose: A Conversation on Tibetan Buddhism and Mystical Christianity (with Lama Tsomo)

For ordering any of these books go to matthewfox.org.

Forward author Ilia Delio, OSF, scientist and theologian, holds the Josephine C. Connelly Endowed Chair in Theology at Villanova University. Among her books are *Christ in Evolution, the Emergent Christ, The Unbearable Wholeness of Being* and *Birth of a Dancing Star.*

Afterward author Rev. Jerry Maynard is an ordained Independent Catholic Priest in the Independent Sacramental Movement and serves in ministry as a Sacred Activist & Community Organizer in Houston, TX. For more information: RevJerryMaynard.org

Ullrrich Javier Lemus painted the cover picture of Thomas Aquinas. See www.ullrrich.com.

Praise for Sheer Joy

"Seizing Aquinas by scapular and capuche, Fox hauls him point by point through the fundamental issues of our day. The introduction is the finest thing on Aquinas I have ever read."

—William Everson, author of The Integral Years and The Residual Years

"This is an important book and will give much pleasure to those looking for deep and richer philosophy."

—New Humanity

"In this book, the teaching of Aquinas come through with a fulness and an insight that has never been represented in English before, and that moreover is shown to have a vital message for the world today. . . . Sheer Joy is a work of major importance not only for the church and the Dominican order but also for the wider world, which is looking for a philosophy that can act as a guide in the moral, social, and political problems of the world today."

—Father Bede Griffiths, author of A New Vision of Reality and Return to the Center

"The sheer joy of the shared commitment of Aquinas and Fox to creation spirituality is contagious and pervades almost every page of this big volume."

—National Catholic Reporter

"Aquinas was what we would now call a holistic thinker, but he went much further than most modern holists in recognizing the all-pervasive influence of the spiritual realm....Until now, Aquinas's insights have been hidden behind a fog of scholastic and neoscholastic commentary and interpretation. This book changes all that. Matthew Fox allows Aquinas to speak for himself, and at the same time the dialogue enables the relevance of what he says to come across with great clarity. After more than seven centuries, we can meet Aquinas again and hear what he has to say to us."

> —Rupert Sheldrake, author of A New Science of Life
> and Science and Spiritual Practices

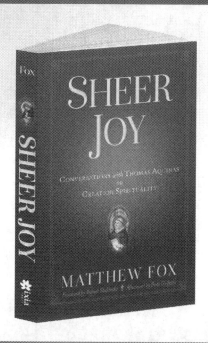

Printed in the United States
By Bookmasters